ISSUE 6

WINTER 2013

for Alli

TABLE *of* CONTENTS

letter from the editors

essays

symposium: what are animals for?

reviews

THE POINT

THE EDITORS	Jon Baskin
	Jonny Thakkar
	Etay Zwick
DESIGN	Marie Otsuka
	Etay Zwick
COVER ART	Matt Vanderzalm
	At the edge of a vast nothingness, 2011
ART EDITOR	Kate Rouhandeh
ASSISTANT EDITOR	Jacob Mikanowski
EDITORIAL CONSULTANT	Gregory Freeman
INTERNS	J. Michael Eugenio
	Claire Withycombe
	Lily Ye
COPY EDITORS	John Colin Bradley
	Lindsay Knight
	Patrick Underwood
EDITORIAL BOARD	Danielle Allen
	Thomas Bartscherer
	Jonathan Lear
	Mark Lilla
	Martha Nussbaum
	Geof Oppenheimer
	Robert Pippin
	Douglas Seibold
	Tom Stern
	Ralph Ubl
ADDRESS	The Point
	732 S. Financial Place, #704
	Chicago, IL 60605
PRINTER	McNaughton & Gunn Inc.
	Saline, Michigan
DISTRIBUTOR	Publishers Group West (PGW)
WEBSITE	www.thepointmag.com

LETTER FROM THE EDITORS:
ON FOOD

I am much more interested in another question,—a question upon which the "salvation of humanity" depends to a far greater degree than it does upon any piece of theological curiosity: I refer to nutrition.

FRIEDRICH NIETZSCHE, *ECCE HOMO*

A human being is primarily a bag for putting food into; the other functions and faculties may be more godlike, but in point of time they come afterwards. A man dies and is buried, and all his words and actions are forgotten, but the food he has eaten lives after him in the sound or rotten bones of his children. I think it could be plausibly argued that changes of diet are more important than changes of dynasty or even of religion. .... Yet it is curious how seldom the all-importance of food is recognized. You see statues everywhere to politicians, poets, bishops, but none to cooks or bacon-curers or market gardeners.

GEORGE ORWELL, *THE ROAD TO WIGAN PIER*

It's hard to imagine civilization without onions.

JULIA CHILD, CHEF

The basic scenario is that we come in from the store and make our little preparations like getting the kettle filled and boiling, and then we lift the lobsters out of the bag or whatever retail container they came home in ... whereupon some uncomfortable things start to happen.

DAVID FOSTER WALLACE, "CONSIDER THE LOBSTER"

Can you really ask what reason Pythagoras had for abstaining from flesh? For my part I rather wonder both by what accident and in what state of soul or mind the first man did so, touched his mouth to gore and brought his lips to the flesh of a dead creature, he who set forth tables of dead, stale bodies and ventured to call food and nourishment the parts that had a little before bellowed and cried, moved and lived. ... It is certainly not lions and wolves that we eat out of self-defense; on the contrary, we ignore these and slaughter harmless, tame creatures without stings or teeth to harm us, creatures that, I swear, Nature appears to have produced for the sake of their beauty and grace. But nothing abashed us, not the flower-like tinting of the flesh, not the persuasiveness of the harmonious voice, not the cleanliness of their habits or the unusual intelligence that may be found in the poor wretches. No, for the sake of a little flesh we deprive them of sun, of light, of the duration of life to which they are entitled by birth and being.

PLUTARCH, MORALIA

Mr. Leopold Bloom ate with relish the inner organs of beasts and fowls. He liked thick giblet soup, nutty gizzards, a stuffed roast heart, liverslices fried with crustcrumbs, fried hencods' roes. Most of all he liked grilled mutton kidneys which gave to his palate a fine tang of faintly scented urine.

JAMES JOYCE, ULYSSES

Sunday dinner isn't sunny.
Easter feasts are just bad luck
When you see it from the viewpoint
Of a chicken or a duck.
Oh how I once loved tuna salad
Pork and lobsters, lamb chops too
Till I stopped and looked at dinner
From the dinner's point of view.

SHEL SILVERSTEIN, "POINT OF VIEW"

Vegetarians, and their Hezbollah-like splinter-faction, the vegans, are a persistent irritant to any chef worth a damn. To me, life without veal stock, pork fat, sausage, organ meat, demi-glace, or even stinky cheese is a life not worth living. Vegetarians are the enemy of everything good and decent in the human spirit.

ANTHONY BOURDAIN, KITCHEN CONFIDENTIAL

Is it not a reproach that man is a carnivorous animal? True, he can and does live, in a great measure, by preying on other animals; but this is a miserable way—as anyone who will go to snaring rabbits, or slaughtering lambs, may learn—and he will be regarded as a benefactor of his race who shall teach man to confine himself to a more innocent and wholesome diet. Whatever my own practice may be, I have no doubt that it is a part of the destiny of the human race, in its gradual improvement, to leave off eating animals, as surely as the savage tribes have left off eating each other when they came in contact with the more civilized.

HENRY DAVID THOREAU, *WALDEN*

The thought of the good pasture and of the calf contentedly grazing flavors the steak. Some, I know, will think it bloodthirsty or worse to eat a fellow creature you have known all its life. On the contrary, I think it means that you eat with understanding and with gratitude. A significant part of the pleasure of eating is one's accurate consciousness of the lives and the world from which food comes.

WENDELL BERRY, *BRINGING IT TO THE TABLE*

A complete lack of caution is perhaps one of the true signs of a real gourmet: he has no need for it, being filled as he is with a God-given and intelligently self-cultivated sense of gastronomical freedom. He not only knows from everything admirable he has read that he will not like Irish whisky with pineapple chilled in honey and vermouth, or a vintage Chambertin with poached lake perch; but every taste bud on both his actual and his spiritual palate wilts in revulsion at such thoughts. He does not serve these or similar combinations, not because he has been *told*, but because he *knows*.

MARY FRANCES KENNEDY FISHER, *AN ALPHABET FOR GOURMETS*

Foodism has taken on the sociological characteristics of what used to be known—in the days of the rising postwar middle class, when Mortimer Adler was peddling the Great Books and Leonard Bernstein was on television—as culture. It is costly. It requires knowledge and connoisseurship, which are themselves costly to develop. It is a badge of membership in the higher classes, an ideal example of what Thorstein Veblen ... called conspicuous consumption. It is a vehicle of status aspiration and competition, an ever-present occasion for snobbery, one-upmanship and social aggression. (My farmers' market has bigger, better, fresher tomatoes than yours.) Nobody cares if you know about Mozart or Leonardo anymore, but you had better be able to discuss the difference between ganache and couverture.

WILLIAM DERESIEWICZ, "A MATTER OF TASTE?"

That eating should be foremost about bodily health is a relatively new and, I think, destructive idea—destructive not just of the pleasure of eating, which would be bad enough, but paradoxically of our health as well. Indeed, no people on earth worry more about the health consequences of their food choices than we Americans do—and no people suffer from as many diet-related health problems. We are becoming a nation of orthorexics: people with an unhealthy obsession with healthy eating.

MICHAEL POLLAN, IN DEFENSE OF FOOD: AN EATER'S MANIFESTO

The only way to keep your health is to eat what you don't want, drink what you don't like, and do what you'd rather not.

MARK TWAIN, FOLLOWING THE EQUATOR

So I commend the enjoyment of life, because nothing is better for a man under the sun than to eat and drink and be glad.

ECCLESIASTES, 8:15

Nothing tastes as good as skinny feels.

KATE MOSS, MODEL

Those who lack experience of knowledge or virtue, but are always occupied with feasts and the like, are brought down, apparently, and then back up to the middle state; and wander in this way throughout their lives, never reaching beyond this to what is truly higher up, never looking up at it or brought up to it, never filled with what really is, and never tasting any stable or pure pleasure. On the contrary, they are always looking downward like cattle and, with their heads bent over the earth or the dinner table, they feed, fatten, and fornicate.

PLATO, REPUBLIC

Worst of all, from this point of view, are those more uncivilized forms of eating, like licking an ice cream cone —a catlike activity that has been made acceptable in informal America but that still offends those who know eating in public is offensive. I fear I may by this remark lose the sympathy of many readers, people who will condescendingly regard as quaint or even priggish the (not-only-Talmudic) view that eating in the street is for dogs. ... Eating on the street—even when undertaken, say, because one is between appointments and has no other time to eat—displays in fact ... [a] lack of self-control: It betokens enslavement to the belly. Hunger must be sated now; it cannot wait. Though the walking street eater still moves in the direction of his vision, he shows himself as a being led by his appetites. Lacking utensils for cutting and lifting to mouth, he will often be seen using his teeth for tearing off chewable portions, just like any animal. Eating on the run does not even allow the human way of enjoying one's food, for it is more like simple fueling; it is hard to savor or even to know what one is eating when the main point is to hurriedly fill the belly, now running on empty.

LEON KASS, *THE HUNGRY SOUL*

Ice-cream is exquisite. What a pity it isn't illegal.

VOLTAIRE, PHILOSOPHER

You can experience [with food] something that is almost the only art form that involves all the senses. With food and dining, I can present you with something audible. I can present you the sense of feeling with different textures. I can show you things that are compelling and shocking and beautiful and exciting. I can make you smell things that evoke memory and create nostalgia and then, after all of that, you get the physiological satisfaction of putting something delicious in your mouth and into your stomach.

GRANT ACHATZ, CHEF

Proust on the madeleine is art; the madeleine itself is not art. A good risotto is a fine thing, but it isn't going to give you insight into other people, allow you to see the world in a new way, or force you to take an inventory of your soul.

WILLIAM DERESIEWICZ, "A MATTER OF TASTE?"

No man can serve two masters: for either he will hate the one, and love the other; or else he will hold to the one, and despise the other. Ye cannot serve God and mammon. Therefore I say unto you, Take no thought for your life, what ye shall eat, or what ye shall drink; nor yet for your body, what ye shall put on. Is not the life more than meat, and the body than raiment?"

GOSPEL OF MATTHEW, 6:24-25

There is nothing to eat,
>   seek it where you will,
>   but of the body of the Lord.
The blessed plants
>   and the sea, yield it
>   to the imagination
intact. And by that force
>   it becomes real,
>   bitterly
to the poor animals
>   who suffer and die
>   that we may live.

WILLIAM CARLOS WILLIAMS, "THE HOST "

She sent for one of those squat, plump cakes called petites madeleines that look as though they have been molded in the grooved valve of a scallop-shell. And soon, mechanically, oppressed by the gloomy day and the prospect of a sad future, I carried to my lips a spoonful of the tea in which I had let soften a piece of madeleine. But at the very instant when the mouthful of tea mixed with cake-crumbs touched my palate, I quivered, attentive to the extraordinary thing that was happening in me. A delicious pleasure had invaded me, isolated me, without my having any notion as to its cause. It had immediately made the vicissitudes of life unimportant to me, its disasters innocuous, its brevity illusory, acting in the same way that love acts, by filling me with a precious essence: or rather this essence was not in me, it was me. I had ceased now to feel mediocre, accidental, mortal. Whence could it have come to me, this all-powerful joy? I was conscious that it was connected with the taste of tea and cake, but that it infinitely transcended those savours, could not, indeed, be of the same nature as theirs. Whence did it come? What did it mean? How could I seize upon and apprehend it?

MARCEL PROUST, SWANN'S WAY

essays

Charles Kerry, *Linda Path, Leura*, circa 1900

A PLEA FOR HUMAN FOOD

by Charles Comey

THE SUMMERS WHEN I was in middle school I spent hiking out West, and we did a lot of putting one foot in front of the other in the most gorgeous places I've ever been. But I don't think that I really walked, or knew what walking was, at that time.

On the other hand, the summer after college when I painted my parents' house, on my days off I would walk from our kitchen door into the woods, pass under the highway via the railroad, and head into a wilderness which, oddly, gets you closer to the city. It was around then that I learned to walk. Maybe it was because it was so unbearably hot that summer, and the only thing you can do in heat like that is wander, and walking is wandering.

I began bird watching that summer, which gives reconnoitering a richness and at the same time floats it in its proper uselessness. That swamp is where you can find the towhees. Over the hill, a line of herons will fly heavily into that flooded bend in the river in the late afternoon. If a walk is going to have a goal it had better be a fanciful one: to revisit a dimly recollected grove of pitch pines and see the extent of the sandy seam they grow in; to see what is just a little further west. No "let's conquer Mt. such and such." That's good when you're with others to avoid the stress of shared decisions, but when you're by yourself you'd better not have such things in mind; you need to be able to make the most of what you encounter, and take an attractive avenue or field opening to the left. Thoreau writes about the paradox of walking: with what he calls sauntering you are always under the impression that just over the horizon is the promised land, and you're always already at home.

The fact that I started to walk in Concord, where I grew up—hallowed New England walking country—obscures an important fact: that the walker is not picky. The walker does not require much. This is why the best walk is one that begins as you step out of your doorway—involve a car and you're unable, unfree, complex and in debt; your feet won't touch the ground.

Walking does, however, require one essential item: you do need a working pair of legs. I was getting really good at walking when something went wrong with my legs. This is what this article is about.

For about half a decade I couldn't walk. In fact I found myself slowing down year by year like the tin man after the rain. The ailment I eventually discovered I had, an autoimmune condition called ankylosing spondylitis (AS)—was baffling to me: constant crippling pain, bones fusing to each other, and, in my case, the threat of dropping dead anywhere anytime. If I had had time to write an essay about this a year ago, when I felt like I was walking waist-deep in water, and the water was pain, it would have been one kind of essay—maybe a better one than I am in a position to write now. It could have been about a phantasmagoria of pharmaceuticals and doctors I'd see for fifteen-minute speed sessions. It could have been an essay about what it is to give up something that you truly love. And it would have been written for my sake much more than for yours.

Instead, however, something really remarkable happened. I departed from my doctors' recommendations—more on that later—and did what was not at all natural to me: I searched around on the internet for information about the disease, and came to find that a group of people with AS claimed to know something simple but very important. There was a problem with what I was eating. They recommended a radical diet that is a lot like the diet man would have eaten before the advent of agriculture. Nine months ago I gave it a try and since then have been, in a word, cured.

So this essay turns out to be about something quite practical. It turns out that almost all of us are not eating food fit for humans. About 72 percent of the food we consume in Western diets comes from sources that were never or very rarely eaten by our ancestors before the last (evolutionarily negligible) 10,000 years. This can make our bodies fall apart, some in small ways, some catastrophically. You or someone you know has these problems or will, which is why you should read this or something like it.

I

BUT I AM getting ahead of my story. Let me begin further back.
One day in his first summer of life our family dog Max went swimming—his bliss—and spent the rest of the summer with red blotches all over his stomach that he'd sleepily shake a paw at. Though my parents thought this would pass, the second summer it happened again, and this time the blotches grew into nasty red continents. He only got sicker into the fall and winter. My parents were referred to a pet allergist, and tests determined that Max was allergic to "*grass, weeds, mosquitoes, trees [a long list of them], feathers, flowers, tobacco, ants, pollen, mites, histamines, horses, cats [!!], sheep, fleas, dust, mold*"—pretty much everything they tested for. Max is blessed with a sweet personality and a lovely coat of hair and this must have helped my parents in the face of the news that their dog's body was so unaccountably unfit for life on Earth. The latter was simply the way it was so far as the vet was concerned, who told them to brace themselves for forking up big bucks for treatment.

Thankfully, just before it was time for this, an acquaintance of my mother's suggested that she try experimenting with what Max was eating. I remember seeing the shiny silver bag of dog food with a woman and her dog romantically silhouetted by an orange and gold sunset over the italicized slogan "*The thinking person's pet food.*" I remember it because it seemed so snobby and also because it sounded a little like the person was going to be eating the pet food. Now, however, the slogan seems to me, whatever else it is, accurate. "*The thinking person's pet food*" appears to imply that the demographic that thinks, thinks profoundly, buys this product. But in fact it might just mean that a dog is an animal that gets sick when it eats grains (which most dog foods are full of), because the ancestors of the dog never ate them and a dog isn't designed to digest them. The thinking being referred to could be just the thinking of this thought.

That at no time in the long descent to dogness did any wild dog eat the seeds of grasses, and that this is one weighty consideration in the question of whether a domestic dog ought to eat them, is an instance of one of the most straightforward post-Darwinian practical principles available to us. At the zoo they don't wait for diet research to roll in before they have an accurate idea of what ought to go into the polar bear compound: they know that this animal eats fish. While a wild diet might not be the last word, it isn't going to lead one far astray. But somehow such reasoning is conspicuously scarce outside the zoo.

The more specific story, we're finding out, is that if a dog eats lots of grains it is prone to developing autoimmunity and allergies and other health problems because it has a compromised intestinal tract that lets antigens into the blood stream. As far as anyone can tell, Max has been hale and fit ever since he started eating his new food. No more horrendous itchy red continents on his underside. At twelve—getting up there as dogs go—he is a lithe blond beast, and swims, when given the chance, for entire afternoons at a stretch. On a recent visit home I found that when Max gets back from a long walk he still sprints a few smooth laps around the house, sending the turf flying.

Max was the first in the family to return to the diet of his forbears. My mother was next. She had some sort of mysterious gastrointestinal issue, and she followed her dog into the past. The human equivalent to the kind of wild-informed diet Max is on is what is now sometimes called an "ancestral," or "archevore," or "cave man" diet, but most often a "Paleo diet," because it tries to mimic man's diet at it was in the long Paleolithic era from 2,600,000 B.C. to 8,000 B.C. when we were hunter-gatherers, when the makeup of our gastro-intestinal system and metabolism were in large part molded. My mother eats a version of a basic Paleo diet: plenty of fish and leafy greens, grass-fed beef, no grains (this covers rice and corn), no legumes (a.k.a. beans), no dairy, no refined oils, little starch, sugar or alcohol.

My own path to a similar diet—not quite a Paleo diet, as I will explain—was rougher than Max's or my mother's. It also involved one big blunder.

NORMALLY IT IS a wonderful thing that we have an immune system. This is the part of our body that seeks out and destroys or disables "antigens"—viruses, harmful microorganisms and other foreign things that have entered the body. We wouldn't survive long in the world without it. But the immune system, we now know, is capable of making mistakes. Some of these are inconvenient but (in most cases) forgivable, like allergies. Allergies are an inappropriate immune response, where one's body comes to see something that is in fact harmless—feathers, etc.—as a threat.

A different kind of mistake that the immune system can make is much more serious. An autoimmune disorder is a disease in which the immune system accidentally slates for destruction some of one's own healthy cells. It is the body's friendly fire, only focused and relentless. This sounds like something exotic—"yes Mr. Bond, the viper's poison will use your body's own defenses to destroy you." So it is. The thing is that today it is more and more common.

Around fifty million Americans, or one in six, suffer from an autoimmune condition, though few people could name one of them with confidence (no, AIDS isn't). We spend around $120 billion on treatment for autoimmunity each year. To give you some perspective, we spend $70 billion on cancer. This isn't counting allergies or asthma, nor well-known diseases such as schizophrenia, Alzheimer's, autism, atherosclerosis or Parkinson's disease, that are now thought to involve autoimmunity.

Now people like to hear about others' health maladies about as much as they like to hear them relate their dreams at the breakfast table. So I'll just tell you where I ended up. After several years—the latter half of my twenties—in which I didn't know what the fuck was happening, I had three big problems. One was that I couldn't sleep. Another was that I experienced excruciating pain in my legs and lower back that unaccountably migrated from place to place. The last and in some ways the most distressing was that a series of echocardiograms, the first of which was supposed to be a routine just-in-case kind of thing for palpitations I had been feeling, determined that my heart was only pumping out about 30 percent of its volume with each beat. A healthy heart pumps 55-60 percent. This kind of heart failure almost always gets worse, and I was in immediate danger of what doctors have given the gentle euphemism "sudden death," where the heart simply stops.

After much meandering from one hypothesis to another, last year I was definitively diagnosed with ankylosing spondylitis. "Spondylitis" means inflammation of the vertebrae, the source of the sufferer's chief complaint. It's really inflammation of the spine and sacrum, and it can also affect other organs like the eyes and, occasionally, the heart. "Ankylos" means bent, referring, I found out, to the disease's most dramatic symptom. Eventually the ligament that runs down the anterior side of the spinal cord calcifies, curling the back into a hardened hunchbacked position. I was diagnosed when an MRI showed the milky beginnings of this process.

Why was my body attacking itself? Immunologists now think that an adequate answer to that question may begin with what was going on in my digestive system. Let me explain what I was eating at the time.

ALTHOUGH I GREW up in Concord, I never really read our local authors until I left—in fact when I arrived at college I hadn't read a word of Emerson, only glimpsed out of the corner of my eye poetry and epigrams etched into stone around town.

Katie Kline, *Williamsburg*, 2010

As for Thoreau, I believe I could have come up with "I went to the woods because I wished to live deliberately" and drawn the lineaments of his cabin. The exception was that I did know what Thoreau said about food: I had had to read it aloud in English class in the tenth grade. (This in lieu of reading the book on our own, our teacher having told us, from experience I suppose, that if we swam out into *Walden* we would drown.)

What I later remembered from the passage I read—it is remarkable how well one remembers what one is responsible for before an audience—was Thoreau's complaint that meat is literally a bloody mess. He says that catching, cooking, etc., his fish takes forever compared to, say, planting potatoes and harvesting them. "The practical objection to animal food in my case was its uncleanness; and, besides, when I had caught and cleaned and cooked and eaten my fish, they seemed not to have fed me essentially. It was insignificant and unnecessary, and cost more than it came to."

When I got to college I finally read *Walden*; in fact I read it more often and more seriously than any other book in my life and it became my good friend; and at that time I didn't drown, I don't think so anyway, I drank up its ideal of simplicity and self-reliance—simplicity as the unappreciated center of the ethics and economics of a responsible life as well as a happy one. I started to try to live up to this in what way I could: taking up the flower over the opera, for the joy of what is wild and gratuitous, not coveted, not sitting on top of grandeur with complex conditions. This, as I understand Thoreau, is one aspect of how to cultivate an ability to take day-to-day undeferred, untriangulated joy in one's life.

I still think that Thoreau is right about that. The point for our purposes here is that when I was twenty or so I became a vegetarian. Meat was complex, complicitous, expensive and unsustainable. Plants grew straight out of the soil—food for someone living lightly.

I was a vegetarian—a good one who really ate lots and lots of vegetables, not a bageltarian—for five years.

VEGETARIANS LIKE TO point to their favorite big vegetarian for evidence that plants can provide all we need for nourishment. Thoreau's example is the ox:

> One farmer says to me: "You cannot live on vegetable food solely, for it furnishes nothing to make bones with"; and so he religiously devotes a part of his day to supplying his system with the raw material of bones; walking all

the while he talks behind his oxen, which, with vegetable-made bones, jerk him and his lumbering plow along in spite of every obstacle.

Strictly speaking Thoreau is quite right: it is possible to make bones out of vegetables. We irresistibly tend to imagine that eating muscle makes muscly men; fat, fat ones. A vegetarian is subjected at Thanksgiving to the inevitable uncle chiding, "you need to put some meat on you" and gesturing to the turkey; and Thoreau is correct: this is more or less fallacious.

On the other hand, it is a terrible idea to draw inferences about nutrition and human health from the diet of the ox. We now know that the process of turning raw material into energy and body structure works quite differently in different animals. An ox is a ruminant. It has four stomachs, the first of which, the "rumen," is designed for digesting grass. This 25-gallon tank contains a huge population of microorganisms that we lack entirely, for breaking down cellulose. It regurgitates its rumen something like 500 times over eight hours to make the most of this extremely nutrient-poor food source—utterly unlike the way we do things.

The example more favored by vegetarians today is the gorilla—much closer to us on the family tree and also a fun one because with the gorilla everyone gets to imagine a leaf-eating silverback playfully pulling one's skeptical meat-stubborn uncle to pieces. The gorilla, however, is what we would have become if we had evolved a survival strategy like that of the ox. Our line of descent diverged from that of the gorilla over seven million years ago, and in that time gorillas acquired cellulose-processing gut flora.

We took our own way. At no point in our long descent to *homo sapiens* did we ever eat grass, as do the gorilla or the ox. Rather we ate the ox, or at least its ancestor the aurochs. To be more specific, we were once tree-dwelling fruitivores. Then the American continents collided, which changed the circulation of warm water worldwide. The heavily forested areas to which our ancestors were adapted gave way to an increasingly open landscape, and it was then—about 2.6 million years ago—that we began a brilliant career as the tool-wielding opportunistic omnivore. We grew a huge hungry brain and a shorter gut designed for quickly digesting rich fatty foods.

We don't know exactly how much meat our hominid ancestors were getting their hands on. Tellingly, modern hunter-gatherer societies take in roughly

65 percent of their calories from animal foods (on average), to our roughly 25 percent. They eat considerably less starch and sugar.*

A LOT OF PEOPLE, myself included, first heard about the ills of carbo-hydrates with the phenomenon of the Atkins diet, and assumed that this began with Atkins. In fact the idea that the volume of carbohydrates consumed in the standard Western diet is harmful to humans has been appreciated for a long time. Among the unexpected revelations that came out of British colonialism in the nineteenth century were the reports that returned from the field regarding the absence of civilization's chief chronic illnesses in pre-agricultural peoples. This came from all corners. Doctors practicing in indigenous non-Westernized populations in Africa, Asia, the South Pacific and America would see plenty of certain sorts of ailments: broken bones, malaria, gangrene. But again and again the doctors observed that a whole range of problems—obesity, cancer, athero-

---

* It is not just Thoreau and vegans that favor spurious animal analogies. Researchers have at times run the analogy the other way: such that if something is bad for another animal, it will be bad for us. It turns out, for example, that when rabbits are force fed cholesterol, they don't do well: they end up with cholesterol in places where no animal is supposed to store the stuff, like their tendons. This grotesque outcome leant early support to the idea that dietary cholesterol causes problematic cholesterol levels in the blood that leads to atherosclerosis and that sort of thing in homo sapiens. The same experiment was subsequently performed on guinea pigs, parrots, pigeons, rats, mice and goats, with the same results.

Never mind that a rabbit's digestive and metabolic arrangement is little like ours. Where the ox has its regurgitation and rumination, the rabbit actually eats its own shit to get the nutrients it needs out of grass. On the other hand, its body is not adjusted to animal foods and has no idea what to do with cholesterol from food.

It turns out that when you try the same experiment on a meat-eater it is a different story. When you force feed a dog cholesterol—and they did—it just wags its tail. And if you draw the inference from what happens to the dog, you get the correct conclusion, which is that consuming choles-terol doesn't significantly raise cholesterol levels in homo sapiens. This, incidentally, is something researchers of all stripes have agreed on since the 1940s. People accidentally mix it up with the idea that saturated fat raises cholesterol levels, and cholesterol in turn is bad for the heart. (If your doc-tor tells you to lay off the eggs because of the cholesterol that they contain you shouldn't see him again: he ought to be able to manage relationships that involve three things). There is scattered and shaky evidence that laying off saturated fat will help your heart health—but let's be clear that that's the only thesis that has actually been on the table.

More recently endocrinologists, who study hormones, are telling us that problems with choles-terol arise for humans, and for dogs, when we consume too many carbohydrates. This is because what is really much more important to us is the 80 percent of the cholesterol that our own bodies synthesize, not the 20 percent we eat, and when we consume too many carbohydrates this appar-ently screws with the system.

sclerosis, asthma, osteoporosis, and a long list of others—were either absent or extremely rare. They were absent, that is, until Western agricultural foods began to be incorporated into the local diet.

It was the same list everywhere, and this led some to call these diet-related diseases "diseases of civilization." In the twentieth century anthropologists leant support to the general idea when they reported that man's dental mass and body stature had diminished with the advent of agriculture.

The fact that the most conspicuous change to our diet after agriculture concerned our intake of starch and sugar was not lost on health profession-als at the time that these discoveries were made. Furthermore the idea that it was carbohydrates, not protein or fat, that were the chief culprit, fit with the evidence that came in from people living with the super-healthy Masai, who eat exclusively blood, milk and meat; or the Inuit, some of whom get close to 99 percent of their calories from animals. To take one example, there was not a single known case of breast cancer anywhere among the Inuit until 1966—and yes, they were looking for it.

In the early twentieth century, however, a competing theory came on the scene very suddenly. Some hypothesized that the diseases of civilization must be related to food abundance, and blamed what they thought was an increase in calorie consumption in general—the theory of the so-called "diseases of affluence." Later many of this persuasion began to focus more specifically on saturated fat.

In the 1960s the medical world was well aware that the evidence that this new theory had going for it—epidemiological evidence comparing the diet and health of (selected) disparate populations—was weak. This was the kind of data that is useful for drawing up fresh, to-be-tested hypotheses, but nothing more than that. Still to be performed, of course, were the rigorous scientific studies. These would be large-scale observation and intervention diet studies within a given population, to test more conclusively, in a controlled way, whether or not it was true that high calorie consumption in general and fat consumption in particular were bad for human health.

The story from here on, as Gary Taubes recounts it in his *Good Calories, Bad Calories*, is an edifying tale of epistemic drift. By the mid 1970s there had been a sort of sea change, and many, including those on record as saying that the more conclusive studies were eagerly anticipated, began acting as though they had already been performed. They had not been performed because they were too expensive. Just a few years later, the idea that fat consumption causes problems like obesity and heart disease had been accepted and canonized so thoroughly that the older hypothesis on starches and sugars was abandoned just because it was so hard to square with it. The rest is history—history that, by way of the 1977 McGovern commission, the FDA's Food Pyramid with its base in spilling bags of golden grains, and a host of institutions and ads and so forth warning of the hazards of fatty foods, led directly to my dim sense that my vegetarianism wasn't just ethically and environmentally right, it was also going to help me live long and lean.

I N THE SPRING of 2005 I began to feel what I at first mistook for a pulled hamstring. This became very painful, and the pain progressed aggressively. Soon I was sort of tottering down the sidewalk, trying to reconstruct how it was that walking was supposed to flow along.

Not long afterwards, pain between my shoulder blades was keeping me up in the middle of the night, and while I was lying in bed I would hear the normal thump-thump ... thump-thump of my heartbeat, but then, occasionally, a thump-thump, thumthi .... THUMP thi .... THUMP thi.... This was what brought me in to discover the heart condition.

In 2005, after the heart diagnosis, I gave up the vegetarianism just in case. I feel now that I could had been much more wise and proactive than that in regard to the role of food. For there was one big diet-related clue I could have picked up on.

It is a peculiarity of mine that when I work intensively at a project, I often sort of forget to eat. When my stomach finally forces me to open the fridge and stretch out my hand for the grapes, I unaccountably veer back to my work by some sort of override. It becomes noon, 1:00, 2:00. The later it gets the more focused I am on the redeeming rendezvous with wisdom that I keep feeling is just now upon me. At 3:00 in the afternoon I will have had nothing but a mug of water.

On such days I would notice that my pain disappeared. At the time I put it down to distraction and adrenaline and the healing heat of creative work. As my brain was being trashed, my body, which by now would be found pacing back and forth from desk to door, was lucid. Sitting at a desk is supposed to make you stiff and ragged, but in comparison to the way I generally felt my body was sailing the floor, floating forward by my gaze.

Reader: if you've got a chronic health issue, especially one that may involve inflammation, try a 24-hour fast. If the symptoms abate you've got good reason to believe it has to do with what you're eating. I didn't make the connection. Given what we now know about AS, this experience makes a lot of sense.

I N **1973** A big advance was made in understanding AS when it was discovered that almost all AS patients share a common gene called HLA-B27. A lot of people have HLA-B27, and only a small proportion of them—about 5 percent—develop the disease. It appears that AS also requires an environmental "trigger" to set it off, which is thought to be true of almost all autoimmune conditions.

Dr. Alan Ebringer is a London immunologist, and the lead protagonist in the story of diet medicine for AS. In 1976 Ebringer reported that he had caught the culprit. A common bowel bacterium named *Klebsiella pneumoniae* looks like the HLA-B26 protein. Ebringer proposed that the two are so similar that the immune system mixes them up.

Today most researchers think the claim that a *Klebsiella* overgrowth causes AS via molecular mimicry is probably overstated at best. But most agree that gut flora is the right place to be looking for AS's pathogenesis.

Gut flora are microorganisms whose environment is the gastrointestinal tract. When we're in the womb our tract is sterile and doesn't harbor any bacteria at all, but as soon as we eat and breathe we begin to seed our own personal populations of these mole people. Then they multiply—if you could extract all of the microorganisms living in your gut and pack them together it would look like a grey-brown softball and weigh about three pounds: upwards of 100 trillion microorganisms, ten times the number of cells in the human body. We are beginning to appreciate what a big influence they have on our health, even if our understanding of the causal connections in play is inchoate.*

In many ways the human body, having evolved in the context of gut microbes, is designed to coexist with them. We give the bacteria a place to live and a steady supply of food, and some of them, the ones we call "probiotics," apparently go to work for us.

---

* The study of gut ecology, or the "microbiome," has taken off in a serious way in the last five years, and is considered to be on the cutting edge of medical science. Among the first lessons learned by the National Institute of Health's ambitious Human Microbiome Project, launched in 2007, has been how unimaginably complex the interrelations of our floral populations are, as well as how radically the makeup of these populations vary from individual to individual.

Although apparently researchers think that the health claims made for yogurt and so forth are premature to put it mildly, many are confident about the prospect of treating a range of diseases—especially those that have been on the rise in the last century—by adjusting the makeup of the microbiome. Treatments that are already being experimented with range from the targeted introduction of bacteria to offset problematic populations, to, taking a page from the Marquis de Sade, "fecal transplants" from healthy donors. Yes, this last has been done, and with remarkable rates of success.

We don't always get along with them, however, and this brings us back to diet. Remember that the human digestive system was set up to handle the kind of food we were eating in the Paleolithic era, and hasn't changed significantly since. People who advocate a Paleo diet think that all sorts of things go wrong—namely the aforementioned "diseases of civilization"—when we stray too far into the modern Western diet. What may be particularly pertinent in my case is that our healthy, predictable relationship with the predictable populations of bacteria in our gut depends on our old, ancestral diet.

Especially problematic in regard to gut flora are starches. Starches are long chains of carbohydrates that have to be "broken down" in the stomach into simple sugars before we can digest them. Unlike simple sugars, which are pretty much always metabolized, about 10-20 percent of the starches we eat remain undigested in the tract and pass into the colon. There they feed bacteria.

Paleolithic man would have encountered starch primarily in a few fruits, vegetables and roots—a relatively small amount. But 10,000 years ago—far, far too recently to have given our DNA any time to adjust—along came agriculture, which is for the most part the cultivation of starch-rich plants for food. Particularly irresistible were grains. The fact that grains are so starchy is in part what makes them reliable, storable, shippable: starchiness is what makes grains a great commodity.

The FDA food pyramid I grew up with had us taking in about 40-50 percent of our calories in the form of starches. This is one of the rare places where American habits have been on par with health recommendations; and as a vegetarian replacing meat with grain products and beans, I was taking in quite a bit more. The result was that my gut flora population—my "microbiome"—was (to put it vaguely, since we lack the details) out of whack.

This, many immunologists now believe, may explain how it is that my body came to attack itself: the constitution of my gut flora was not to my body's liking, and my body, attempting to beat back an infestation, ended up accidentally attacking the healthy cells in my spine, sacrum, heart and who knows what else.

II

IN 2009 I was finally diagnosed with AS. Even then, however, I remained in the dark about the possible role of diet in the disease. Once you have

Debbie Carlos, *Leek Soup*, 2011

a diagnosis for AS you are referred to a rheumatologist. Mine looked like a battle-hardened wrinkly witch, but she didn't turn out to be as interesting as she looked. She took me into her office and breezily went over the basics of AS, holding up a plastic chart of what looked like a schema of WWII battleships and were actually anti-inflammatory pills. Five months later I had tried three of these and felt quite a bit worse. I called to find out what I should do and was told that next in her "big bag of tricks"—these were her assistant's words, though it didn't seem like a big bag to me—was to begin immunosuppressant infusions.

This was what was on my mind a year ago. The general public doesn't know much about autoimmune diseases, but investors do. The immunosuppressant drug Humira is set to become the most lucrative pharmaceutical in the world in 2012. Drugs like Humira run a patient $15,000-25,000 per year and higher. Because immunosuppressants knock back the body's defense system as a whole, they also make you more susceptible to serious infections, cancer, congestive heart failure and liver disease, to name just some of their side effects. Nevertheless they are hailed as a miracle by doctors, and for good reason: they are often the last line of treatment for otherwise debilitating pain and degeneration, and can give a patient who has been suffering for years profound relief within weeks. They have a positive effect on AS symptoms about half the time.

On the same day I learned that immunosuppressants were next up for treatment options, I remember my wife seeing me struggling to lean over to unload the dishwasher and saying: "Oh just go lie down." It looked like I was probably going to need to give immunosuppressants a try, though this couldn't be entered into lightly because apparently they can be hard to get off of once you're on them.

First, though, I thought I should try fiddling with my diet. By this time, as I've related, both my mom and Max were on ancestral foods. Also a friend of mine was a proselytizing "Paleo person" with his own blog. I remember Paul at Thanksgiving picking up a huge turkey leg and gnawing on it. Unconvinced that there would be enough dark meat to satisfy his need for fat, he had shown up with his own personal duck. Paul looked like he was consuming about three times more calories than the rest of us which to be frank I found disturbing, but I had to admit he was acting about three times more vigorous than I was feeling. Where was the usual Chicago grad student late November pallor? So I had one big advantage that you, reader, may not enjoy: seeing is believing.

(Incidentally Paul also once told me that it is a good idea to sit for an entire week doing nothing at all when the mood comes upon one, which he figured was what it was like for cavemen back in the day from time to time.)

It was with my inquiries into the future of Paul's heart health, and his responses to them, that I first began to pay attention to the history regarding fats and dietary recommendations I've related above. Today the large scientific studies anticipated in the 1960s are actually beginning to roll in, and by and large the results do not tend to support the idea that saturated fat is bad for you. What continues to pile up is the evidence that starches and sugars at the levels we're consuming them can be very dangerous. For lots of people, this leads to insulin issues. For others a Western diet, and especially grains, may have the effect of damaging the digestive tract, and causing what is called "increased intestinal permeability." The end result of increased intestinal permeability is that we fail to properly screen things that pass into the bloodstream, making the whole unfortunate molecular mimicry cascade to autoimmunity that much more likely, just because there is so much more for the immune system to fight and make mistakes with. And then there are the gut floral issues I have described.

Long before I knew I had AS, Paul had mentioned that a Paleo diet alleviates autoimmunity in some people. When I got my diagnosis I remembered the claim. So then, really as a way to sort of prepare myself for a life on immunosuppressants, I decided to experiment with a Paleo diet just to be sure, for the purpose of eliminating everything but the immunosuppressants I guess you could say.

This was in December of 2011. Doing a little research on my new diet quickly led me to a blog by a guy who had AS and said that as everyone knows the key with AS isn't quite Paleo, but a diet that eliminates all starches. So I switched my dietary test to that instead. I thought it would most likely be a temporary thing—I'd give it two weeks.

THE IDEA THAT you could effectively get over active AS by eating less starch wasn't immediately obvious, even to those that initially proposed the gut flora connection. Fortunately, at this point serendipity stepped in. A patient of Dr. Ebringer's who saw him for AS in the early 1980s asked him if he had any advice for losing weight. Ebringer, for reasons that had nothing to do with arthritis and autoimmunity—and departing, obviously, from the opinions of the time—recommended a diet of red meat and tomatoes. The patient took the advice and did lose weight, but more importantly he also came back reporting something shocking: his pain and inflammation were gone as well.

A light went on in Ebringer's mind: these foods don't contain complex carbohydrates. The starch must be what feeds the relevant gut flora; and gut floral overgrowth must not be a one-time passing "trigger" for AS but an ongoing cause and condition of its pathology. This means that we can treat AS by reducing the starch we take in. Ebringer came up with what he called the "London AS Low-Starch Diet," which he administered to patients at his clinic. This basically consisted of four prohibitions: NO BREAD, NO POTATOES, NO CAKES (in Britain this comprehends pastries), NO PASTA. He published his findings on the diet in a 1996 paper, which reported that of the 450 patients he treated at his clinic in London between 1983-1996, over half now required no medication. His clinical intervention trial of 36 patients showed a statistically significant decline in markers for inflammation over a period of nine months.

In effect, the idea behind the diet is that eating less starch has the same result as my accidental fasts: it starves out certain gut flora, this time by more precisely targeting their starchy substrate. Bacteria are notoriously hard to eradicate entirely but they do die without sustenance. Whether or not Ebringer turns out to have been correct regarding the role of the *Klebsiella* organism specifically, it appears that he discovered how to change the constitution of one's gut flora in such a way as to curtail AS autoimmunity.

The Spondylitis Association of America, the largest disseminator of information to AS patients in the world, until recently made the very visible and important claim on their website regarding Ebringer's findings that "other studies ... have found that the diet has little or no effect on symptoms." When I ran across this statement, I contacted them to find out more. What followed was an exchange of emails in which I basically asked over and over "but what studies specifically?" They ended up dropping the claim from the site. Because, as they then found, there have been no such studies.

Why the SAA made such a stark and egregious error I'm not sure. (To their credit they amended it quickly). Why no one in the medical world other than Ebringer and his colleagues has touched the diet, and indeed no large-scale intervention diet studies have ever been performed on AS patients, and instead rheumatologists pooh pooh the very idea of diet-based medicine in spite of mounting consensus among researchers regarding the role of intestinal health and gut flora, is a different discussion for a different time.

THE IDEA OF treating AS with a diet low in starches could have languished in Ebringer's ignored 1996 paper, and shed no light on the likes of me, if it weren't for the excitement and evangelism of Ebringer's healed patients, and later those influenced by them (this essay, for example, being my contribution).

By the late 1990s those who had their legs back because of Ebringer's diet connected his work to two of the diet's present-day heroes. First, someone discovered that there was already a book on eating starch-free called *The IBS Low-Starch Diet* by a layperson named Carol Sinclair. Sinclair had discovered, after much tinkering and testing, that she could cure her irritable bowel if she proscribed all starch. Her regimen is much more thorough than Ebringer's rather low-key prohibitions, and today her book is the main how-to treatise for people like me who are on a strict "No Starch Diet," or NSD. Sinclair recently discovered via genetic testing that she had AS all along.

The other individual Ebringer's patients connected with was an AS sufferer the no starch community knows as Dragonslayer. Dragonslayer is NSD's apostle to the internet, the co-founder and owner of kickas.org, the main forum for information on the diet. Dragonslayer has the quirk of capitalizing the word "you," and when provoked by NSD skeptics he uses words like "demise" and "downfall" in sentences that sound like they should be followed by "mwaha-hahaha," e.g. "*And with every statement, You crawl further out on the limb You are sawing off.*" "*NONSENSE! You might want to re-read the study and pay attention this time. There may be a quiz at the end.*" Since kickas.org went online in 1999, Dragonslayer reports that he has personally helped over two hundred people to remission through NSD via his online correspondence—which if it's accurate is an astonishing achievement for a layman who never sought to make a penny from it. The night that I began the diet I read Dragonslayer's "NSD QuickStart and tips." While in general I try to avoid throwing away my sunny days on the internet like I'm slack-lipped at a rummage sale, this easy ability to share and glean information outside the orthodox medical community radically improved, and maybe saved, my life. I could not be more thankful to those who made the diet a presence online.

III

I N READING WHAT I am about to describe, you must remember that my intention is not to convince you to try a draconian diet like mine. Such things are for gimps such as myself. I'm trying to convince you to lean toward our hominid past and thus avoid autoimmunity as well as other diet-related diseases, which together affect 50-65 percent of people eating a contemporary Western diet worldwide.

Some of the things that NSD prohibits: all grains (which includes wheat, which of course means pastries, pasta, etc.; also corn and corn products, rice); all legumes; all root vegetables; a few fruits (like bananas); and certain nuts, including peanuts (anyway they're peas not nuts).

Some things are tricky and their starchiness has to be determined item by item. For this I use an old middle school chemistry class trick I learned from Sinclair's *The IBS Low-Starch Diet*: iodine turns blackish blue if you put a droplet on something starchy. All tomatoes need to be tested in this way. So do apples, vine fruits like watermelons, and coconuts.

That leaves one with all animal foods, most fruits and vegetables, and the remaining nuts. People on NSD can eat dairy, which makes the diet in this one sense more permissive than one that sticks strictly to Paleolithic foods.

This is all, needless to say, an immense pain in the ass. In the first weeks that I was eating the food of the hunter-gatherer, I felt a bit like a hunter-gatherer must have felt in a world where food was hiding and had to be ferreted out from the rocks. At the supermarket I soon found it was not worthwhile to venture into the actual aisles of the store, since almost everything that can be found there is starchy or has had starch added to it. I had to stick to the periphery. There is often literally nothing I can eat at gas stations.

As I say, initially I was sure this was just a two-week experiment. I would soon return to my old diet, the diet of my friends, family and neighbors. I thought it most likely that the online NSD people were willful witnesses and hypochondriacs. Right around two weeks in, however, when my trial was to conclude, I started to feel significantly better in my legs and back, and I understood that this was for real.

The community on kickas.org has built up an edifice of anecdotal info: it appears that the no starch diet doesn't work for all AS sufferers, and it works best in those that catch the disease early. Relief arrives in two to ten weeks or so (it isn't as immediate as fasting), and the pain will stay away unless you eat starch, in which case you are likely to get a "flare up" of symptoms. You need to be really rather strict with the diet it for it to work well: a bite of yogurt that contains corn starch will set you back.

The latter has indeed been my experience. Diets like mine are very difficult, and I wish I could congratulate myself on the kind of rare restraint that often has to go into such things. The truth is that I open the cupboard at my wife's parents' place and am presented with food that will put me into face-altering pain within five hours. This will last two or three days. Whatever respecting that is, it cannot be called restraint.

Charles Comey, *Breakfast*, 2012

I T TOOK TWO weeks for me to see results, which was very motivating. But the diet of course took much longer to get accustomed to. In the end, what had to happen was a kind of reimagining of what was reasonable in regard to eating meat, and especially fat, and also a sort of magnification in my mind of foods I was already familiar with.

This morning when I got downstairs I sliced a sausage in half and fried it. Once it was almost done I drained off the fat and heaped in baby spinach so that this stuck out over the top of the pan. The result looks like two brownish-gold submarines in weeds. I keep poached eggs in ramekins in the fridge, and I heated two of these in the microwave with some butter (this is how restaurants do it—happily it's quite delicate). I put blackberries around the edge of the plate.

For a long time I don't think I quite realized that this or something like it was now to be an every-morning thing for me. It still felt like a once-a-month brunch. Incidentally, however, in this country, right up into the late nineteenth century, for those who could afford it this was a standard morning meal: Thoreau's contemporaries very often ate a breakfast of eggs and meat much like mine. A meal of boiled grains such as farina would be the last resort of the poor, one of Dickens's symbols for their suffering.

Actually American expectations in regard to breakfast have a rather dubious history, one worth recounting now, as I'm sure, reader, you're thinking that I've started to stray beyond the bounds of what's reasonable.

The story of dry grains and our notion that they're the healthy way to begin the day got its start in religious radicalism. In the early nineteenth century, a Presbyterian minister by the name of Graham, namesake of the cracker, began to promote a high-fiber vegetarian diet as a way to curb carnal passions. He was especially obsessed with "self-abuse," what they used to call masturbation. People had believed for a long time that a diet that excludes meat, the diet of the holy ascetic, reduces libido. Today there is actually a lot of evidence to back up that claim. In the nineteenth century with people like Graham, however, there emerged the erroneous notion that sexual arousal was itself terrible for our health—the problem, so he wrote, at the root of most modern ailments. So the vegetarian diet was not just the most spiritually pure diet, but the healthiest human diet too.

Graham influenced those who went on to radically change our culinary habits. Among them was the founder and head of the Seventh Day Adventist church, Ellen White. The Seventh Day Adventists are best known for their belief that Saturday is the Sabbath. They also have a very literal interpretation of Genesis 1:29: "Behold, I have given you every herb bearing seed ... to you it shall be meat." They are vegetarians. For religious reasons they believe that man is not supposed to eat meat. Now Graham and his followers were conveniently adding that this vegetarianism is best for the body as well as the soul. White and the Adventists founded a sanitarium in Battle Creek, Michigan, "The San"— the setting and subject of the 1993 comic bestseller *The Road to Wellville*—to promote the new health principles, and appointed their fellow parishioner and physician John Harvey Kellogg to run it.

Dr. Kellogg had the charisma and commercial savvy that Graham lacked. He shared with Graham an abhorrence of sexuality. In his manual on avoiding sexual arousal and activity, *Plain Facts For Old and Young*, Kellogg describes the procedures he used for preventing masturbation at The San:

> The prepuce, or foreskin, is drawn forward over the glans, and the needle to which the wire is attached is passed through from one side to the other. After drawing the wire through, the ends are twisted together, and cut off close. It is now impossible for an erection to occur.

Quite simple really. And there was something for the ladies: "In females, the author has found the application of pure carbolic acid (phenol) to the clitoris an excellent means of allaying the abnormal excitement." Kellogg was a piece of work. When he couldn't cure someone, he would accuse them of masturbation. He himself was married but celibate, penning parts of *Plain Facts* on his wedding night. He would have an assistant give him an enema every morning after breakfast.

It was Kellogg who bequeathed to us the reason still given for the healthfulness of dry cereals: that they cleanse us. Really everything Kellogg did was in one way or another about cleansing. He spent much of the latter half of his life coming up with ways to purify the white race (some sort of scheme involving nuts). At the top of Kellogg's list for avoiding the arousal of the blood in carnal lust and its attendant maladies was bland, high-fiber vegetarian food, especially dry cereal grains, which would pass through the intestines and rake out matter that he thought stimulated the genitals. At this time, with The San at the middle of the action, many of the dry cereals that we know today and that still command a lot of shelf space at the supermarket were developed and marketed: shredded wheat, granola, bran and corn flakes. All were given the same recommendation: that they would keep us clean. Shredded wheat actually looks (and tastes—as Kellogg himself noted) like a bristle brush.

In the twentieth century a lot of fiber-rich dry foods like breakfast cereals and crackers had the fiber processed out of them to make them tastier (Graham would have shaken his head at the sugary sweet fate of the Graham cracker, which basically became a cookie). The scrubbing action of fiber was ripe for a new revival, and that revival—again led by religious men, this time two British missionary doctors, Denis Burkitt and Hugh Trowell—is what we're still living through.

But aren't I committing a genetic fallacy here? However misguided its beginnings, surely the benefits of fiber have now been backed up by modern dietary research? Actually no. Not even close. In the 170 years since the cereal revolution, very few controlled clinical or large-scale observation studies of dietary fiber from grains have ever been performed—seriously—and in those that have the results have been dismal. As Gary Taubes writes of the hypothesis that fiber is important for human health: "The pattern is precisely what would be expected of a hypothesis that simply isn't true: the larger and more rigorous the trials set up to test it, the more consistently negative the evidence." For fiber, as with anti-fat recommendations, the royal road ran from hypothesis to advertising to accepted health doctrine, without making a stop at meaningful, rigorous research. Only now is that research beginning to roll in. On one point the fiber enthusiasts appear to be correct: fiber does lead to more "regularity" and bigger poops—the obsession of octogenarian weirdoes. The trouble is that we have yet to find any correlation between bowel regularity and a single significant mark of human health, including colon cancer.

The data on fiber isn't conclusive yet, but by all appearances fiber is going the way of the douche. We used to think that a lot of other things needed to be cleaned: vaginas, veins, throats, ears, sinuses. If there's a hole, someone has thought that it would be a good idea to get up in there regularly and go to work. With all of these most of us have returned to the common sense idea—having, today, perhaps a little more trust in the body—that the inaccessible insides of an animal will generally do a fine job keeping tidy on their own.

Pretty much everything Kellogg did at The San has turned out to be arrant quackery. What hangs on is our prejudice as to what's for breakfast. Kellogg was also a leader in the new formula that set the standard for making money in food development in the next century and a half. Basically big business in marketing food has to focus on what it can commodify and brand. It's not easy to do this with my breakfast—eggs, sausage, spinach, blackberries—at least not in a proprietary way. You can brand things that you've changed, cooked up, modified to make edible, and you can commodify what you can store and ship. This you can give a name like "Grape Nuts." "Grape Nuts," neither grape nor nut, was invented by C.W. Post, one of Kellogg's patients at The San and another deplorable mix of religious fervor, charlatanry and commercial savvy.

Interestingly there is one thing Dr. Kellogg may have gotten right: he appears to have been ahead of his time in his speculation that many modern ailments have to do with intestinal flora. Only he thought that this should be treated by eating bristle brush-like substances, and the liberal application of yogurt up the butt.

It so happens that one paper I've seen cited in the context of AS and gut flora is a 1973 study of 47 contemporary Seventh-Day Adventists. The vegetarian Adventists had on average 30,000 *Klebsiella* organisms per gram in their feces—the organism that may cause AS via molecular mimicry—compared to 700 organisms per gram in the controls on a normal mixed American diet: in other words, these vegetarians had more than forty times the amount of this microbe in their gut.

There have to date been no epidemiological studies on the link between vegetarianism and autoimmune disease, though many suspect one. For what it's worth all four of the people I know with an autoimmune disorder, including myself, were vegetarians in their youth—tragically two still are.

FIGURING OUT BREAKFAST, or I guess you could say allowing it, was one of the first big adjustments I had to make on the diet. There are plenty of things that I still miss, of course. One that seizes me from time to time is that without starches, there are very few things that I can eat that are crunchy. Not a chomp like a cucumber but a dry crackly crunch—apparently one of the few food sensations a baby doesn't have to learn to like. I recently baked kale chips purely for crunch, but when I bit into them they made a crinkle.

In general, however, I've found that I've made a good bargain when it comes to delight and satisfaction in food: starch and sugar for fat. And there is nothing in the diet that is like choking on a bran muffin.

Thoreau, a lax vegetarian, a vegetarian "in his imagination," as he says, lets fly in one of *Walden*'s many parrhesic paragraphs:

> As I came home through the woods with a string of fish, trailing my pole, it being now quite dark, I caught a glimpse of a woodchuck stealing across my path, and felt a strange thrill of savage delight, and was strongly tempted to seize and devour him raw; not that I was hungry then, except for that wildness which he represented. Once or twice, however, while I lived at the pond, I found myself ranging the woods, like a half-starved hound, with a strange abandonment, seeking some kind of venison which I might devour, and no morsel could have been too savage for me.

The reformed vegetarians I know have some such story to tell. My recollection, which I suppose is the other side of Thoreau's, is of approaching home across the park below my apartment with numb fingers on a raw February night, looking up at my windows where my wife was cooking and knowing in my heart that no soybean would warm my extremities.

One wonders about Thoreau. *Walden* is his long paean on the ills of cultivation and civilization in favor of the primitive and the wild—the mock-Georgic agricultural chapter "The Bean Field" not at all excepted. He explains that he is "less and less a fisherman" because he is learning to heed an intuition. He says of this: "It is a faint intimation, yet so are the first streaks of morning." What he leaves hanging is why he heeded what was so faint, and why he didn't find a place for his other much less faint feelings.*

For lunch today I have brought to work some leftover beef tips and salad, supplemented by rolled-up turkey cold cuts with mustard, olives, and summer squash. I have an apple for a snack (a Fuji—one of the few reliably non-starchy varieties), and a chunk of chocolate.

I have taken to making a batch of crab cakes on the weekend. When I get home tonight I will probably have a pre-dinner snack of one of these. For dinner it's wild salmon, of which I will serve myself about three times as much to eat in one sitting as I did last summer.

T HE QUESTION "WHAT ought we to eat?" involves not just nutritional considerations, but also ethical, environmental, and pecuniary ones. These after all were the considerations that led me to my vegetarianism all those years. Where have I put them? I'll try to be open about what still unsettles me.

The truth is that whereas I remember a time when my wife and I budgeted $150 per week on groceries for the two of us—about average for an American household—now it is more in the range of $220. I bite the bullet on spending significantly more money on what I eat now. We've cut back on other things like dining out and, happily, health bills.

If you can't afford it, well then this just isn't an option obviously; but there are different degrees of "can't" here. As late as the 1940s, Americans allocated more than 40 percent of their income to food. Something that it is important

---

* I can't help noting that Thoreau died at 44, ostensibly of TB. TB is an infectious disease, but many suspect that there is a connection between TB and autoimmunity, as the two are strongly correlated.

to recognize is that the reason we are now able to allocate so little—around 15 percent, including eating out—is that such low prices are sustained by conditions that must change: cheap fossil fuels, abuse of an immigrant work force, and especially the once rich but now increasingly depleted and desiccated soil of the Midwest. In the case of factory-farmed meat, prices are kept low by our tolerance of the animals' abominable anguish and misery.

My diet has me buying grass-fed beef and bison and other animal foods raised down the road in New Hampshire where I live (which, like much of the rest of the planet, isn't suitable for grain agriculture anyway). That is what much of my high expenditure is going toward. There's little that I'm confident about in regard to the social responsibility of my diet, but there is no question, on this one matter, that the pasture is a better life for the cow.

The pasture may also be preferable environmentally. Unlike a cow on a feed lot, what a pastured cow consumes is transformed, firstly, into cow, and then the remainder comes back to the soil as nitrogen-rich pee and manure. The ruminant is part of a process that turns renewable resources—sunlight and rain—into both nutritious food and fertility, the same fifty-million-year-old ecology that built up the rich topsoil of the world's agricultural areas. It does so largely without the intervention of fossil fuels.

This last point is often passed over. Some of our reflexes when it comes to the social irresponsibility of carnivorism come from the fact that when we compare eating meat to eating vegetables, and impressively add up how many more people can be fed on an acre of soybeans and so forth, we are often obliviously talking about agriculture that draws on various forms of nonrenewable natural capital. One such source, the prairie soil, was actually made from generations of the resident ruminants that the soybeans are said to be preferable to. The truth is that intensive agriculture in the absence of livestock either enters endgame or depends heavily on fertilizers that are themselves made with, and from, fossil fuels. You may have heard that in many agricultural areas aquifers are depleted (read: no water), and the cracking, wizened-white soil is washing away. Increasingly the soil that the world's grains come from is literally dead, with none of the biotic vitality required for plant life but pumped-in fertilizers.

In *The Omnivore's Dilemma*, Michael Pollan estimates that an acre of corn takes fifty gallons of oil all told to come to table. There may or may not be a catastrophe resulting from a serious hike in the price of fossil fuels, but it isn't clear to me which food choices will do a better job of averting or assuaging it.

Feeding everyone on spangled cows in a grassy dale with wet nostrils open to the breeze, and fish from the deep blue ocean, is not in the cards. I have no illusions that the hardest question—one certainly on my mind—is one I'm only further from an answer to: What about the whole world? The distressing truth as far as I can tell is that comparing, say, responsibly raised animal foods to grains, the choice is between food that is viable but hardly high-yield enough for all, or a food we can (and do) grow for the whole world, using up resources we're rapidly running low on. Without the use of fossil fuels for fertilizer, our planet has a human carrying capacity of around four billion. We're at seven billion. That's an untidy constraint I have no idea what to do with when something in me inarticulately wants to know how the whole world and its children's children can live, and wants to live like that.

MEANWHILE IT DOES seem obvious to me which is the correct choice nutritionally. Five years ago my cardiologist told me I wasn't likely to live a long life. One year ago I was told that in the event I did live a long life I might not be able to look my friends and family in the eye, because even if treatment for AS went well it was likely that my sacrum and spine all the way up to my skull would be gradually fusing into one bent bone.

And I was in a lot of pain. It is hard to describe the way it feels to have inflammation in the hip area. It doesn't feel like there is some spot that hurts. Rather it's like as long as you stay still the world will keep its normal laws, but take a step and a different dimension flickers on, and there is no possibility of understanding how it works. It's like you're trying to move in an anti-medium, a thickening thing, pain, with the slow awkwardness of an underwater Kung Fu scene. I also had insomnia for those years, which may or may not have been related to autoimmunity.

Two weeks after I began to eat a no starch diet my pain pretty much went away—from like a 4 or a 5 every day with no remission for the final two years to a 1. I also began to sleep well. Three months in, my inflammation had crept back to its deepest strongholds; I didn't feel pain anymore unless I poked really, really hard in one spot on my tailbone. Then one day that too was gone. Today, nine months in, I'm fine, and I can jog and so forth like old times. At my most recent (and I'm hoping my last) visit to the rheumatologist my blood work showed my indicators for inflammation were normal—low, in fact, as Americans go.

Over the years my heart had mysteriously been improving its function bit by bit. Originally the cardiologist told me that this couldn't happen, but she and I watched as my heart went from pumping out 30 to 35 to 40 to 45 percent, with each semiannual echocardiogram from 2007-2010. I became glad I declined the invasive internal defibrillator that she had prescribed. Of course I can't be sure what caused this recovery, but my best guess is that when I was tested at 30 percent I had, as I have recounted, been a vegetarian for five years. At my most recent visit to the cardiologist, five months into the no-starch diet, the echocardiogram showed my heart pumping out 55 percent of its volume with each beat—in other words, normal. The report literally says "all valves working normally."

If I had assented to what the experts I saw prescribed to me in the half-decade before I began the diet, I would have a device the size of a cigarette box implanted in my chest with permanent wires running into my heart. This would be liable, scandalously often it turns out, to give me a shock without warning when it isn't needed. There is no off switch. One poor guy, I learned, had it misfire on him 74 times in one day.

I would today be on anti-inflammatories, antidepressants (I was soon to begin these to treat the insomnia), and needling myself each week for dangerous immunosuppressant infusions. I don't think that any of these recommendations were out of the ordinary; I sought out and got some of the best help available.

I was so close to this fate—really if any one of the parts of the story of the no starch diet and its dissemination, or any one of the factors leading me to try it, hadn't played out, I would be on all of these treatments. And I would be lethargic from the unreal sleep afforded by pharmaceuticals. And I would most likely still be in a lot of pain. And fusing up. Then there would be other costs. The defibrillator would have cost my insurance $50,000 (of which I would pay ten percent), with a $5,000 new battery every five years. The immunosuppressants would be running $15-25,000 per year, to say nothing of all the continued exams, visits to specialists, surgery. I would be journeying into a dark, dependent and bewildering life. Now, instead, I'm quite well. That's the bottom line in my personal story.

I F YOU PERUSE the health columns in the *New York Times*, you'll see that the titans are rebelling: pissed off Salt, Saturated Fat, and Cholesterol are re-ascending Mt. Olympus. Waify Stretching has just been cast down the rocks. They've got blond Grains in their arms and are heaving him back and forth, winding up for the blissful banishing toss.

Next month you'll see columns cheering on the old order. This sort of twenty-first century fog of data can make any attempt to address one's health by diet feel like guesswork. But I think what I am suggesting is a straightforward idea. When archaeologists and anthropologists can tell us that hominids ate such and such, then this food is probably fine; and when they tell us that hominids never ate such and such, or very little of it, there is good reason to suspect it isn't—because we are hominids. Given that hominids historically rarely ate grains, for example, we shouldn't eat them in mass quantities. By no means is that an air-tight rubric; but it's a good general guideline, to be followed in a way one finds reasonable.

Hippocrates is supposed to have said "Let food be your medicine and medicine be your food." That's for the afflicted. For ordinary people it ought to be: make sure your food is food for the kind of thing that you are. Michael Pollan's now famous definition of food is that it is only food if your grandmother would recognize what it is. The idea of eating like our ancestors, at least the version of it I take up, is something similar: it is human food if your great-great-grandmother out to about 150 generations was eating it.

HIPPOCRATES IS ALSO supposed to have said: "Walking is man's best medicine," and in this he and I are most firmly in agreement.

Last April my son Ben was born, our first. Those first few weeks stretch people pretty thin. It's hard to know what it would have even looked like if my insomnia and inflammation were still around then. By April, however, I was in full remission from the disease, and I was able to be the legs of the family while my wife recovered from the birth.

I take care of Ben in the morning, and every day I strap him into his sort of backpack and we take a meandering walk, if a modest one. There is a 50 percent chance that Ben inherited the HLA-B27 gene from me, but hopefully there will be no need to ever find out. He and my wife will eat—what becomes inevitable with me eating the way I do—a sharply starch-reduced diet, and if the account I've laid out here is correct then there's not much chance of him developing the disease in our house. I'm hoping that his dad will get stronger and stronger as he grows up.

Ryan Walach, *Scream*, 2012

OUT WITH THE NEW

SIMON REYNOLDS'S *RETROMANIA*

by Ben Jeffery

They had found their affinity in art, in a love for what art promised and a hatred for where those promises stopped, for the separate and privileged realm society reserved for beautiful, impotent dreams—but even the beauty, they thought, had been a lie for thirty years, before any of them had been born. Somewhere ... art burned itself out in a war against its own limits, in a struggle to escape its redoubt, its museum, its amusement park, its zoo; since then there had been no art, only "imitations of ruins" in a "dismal yet profitable carnival, where each cliché had its disciples, each regression its admirers, every remake its fans."

GREIL MARCUS, *LIPSTICK TRACES: A SECRET HISTORY OF THE TWENTIETH CENTURY*

WHILE I WAS reading Simon Reynolds's latest book, *Retromania: Pop Culture's Addiction to Its Own Past*, I found myself thinking of the hours I spent as a teenager listening to grunge rock in my best friend's bedroom. This would have been somewhere between 2001 and 2005, and so about a decade after the heyday of Nirvana, Pearl Jam and those other groups loosely associated with Seattle, plaid shirts and MTV in the early Nineties. My friend is part of a family which was, and remains, extremely close to mine. The two of us are the same age and he has two older brothers and a sister. My own parents' interest in rock ended, more or less, with *Sgt. Pepper's Lonely Hearts Club Band*, and I'm an eldest child, so I never had a big brother or sister to inherit albums from. But in the other family there was a lineage: what the dad (an amateur jazz agent, among other things) and the older siblings liked would filter down and eventually, almost by diffusion, pass on to me. Grunge wasn't all we listened to; it wasn't even the main thing we listened to—that would have been classic rock of one stripe or another—but it's grunge that comes to mind most vividly now. Grunge was what elder brothers and sisters listened to; it was also the birth of that semi-oxymoronic concept of mainstream "alternative" rock that became the paradigm for so many other guitar bands over the next two decades. Even before I knew much about them I had the idea that Nirvana's success was an event. Whether or not you even *liked* the music all that much (and by now the only album from that time that I still have much affection for is Alice in Chains's *Dirt*) it felt important and interesting in a way that barely needed to be explained.

Anybody's taste is an accident, and at all ages the stuff you happen to like is rarely as important as you think it is (although this is *emphatically* the case when you're a teenage boy). But preferences are always more than accidents, too, connected as they are to great webs of history and culture—individualized symptoms of forces you might not have the slightest idea of. "Easy to forget just how utterly unexpected Nirvana's breakthrough was," writes Reynolds in *Bring the Noise* (2007), an anthology of his articles about rock and hip-hop:

> I remember arriving in New York early in the autumn of 1991 to stay with my girlfriend/wife-to-be, and Joy saying, "There's this video ['Smells Like Teen Spirit'] MTV are playing, it's *amazing*, you've *got* to see it..." And then being slightly incredulous when she said it was by Nirvana (what, that nothing-special group on Sub-Pop?). And then being totally blown away. Along with the sheer power of the song and the brilliance of the video, the shellshock came from the fact that we'd never thought that sound—which came out of all our 1980s faves, Husker Du and Dinosaur Jr. and the Pixies—had any chance of entering the mainstream, let alone taking it over. The major labels had tried their best, and by 1990 had even signed flagrantly uncommercial underground outfits like Butthole Surfers and Sonic Youth. There'd be a very slight sense of critical mass building (Jane's Addiction's success and then Lollapalooza in the summer of '91), of something swarming outside the barricades. But nobody expected the walls to come tumbling down—least of all the bands themselves.

Nirvana arrived like an eruption—a roar in the midst of, and against, the staid mainstream. ("The only explanation is that a lot of people didn't realize how angry and alienated they really were," Reynolds observed at the time.) Despite not being particularly innovative, one thing that distinguished Nirvana from older system-shocks like Elvis or Beatlemania or punk was that the music all these kids were suddenly identifying with was an expression of profound self-hatred and impotence. Why this should have struck such a chord in pre-Millennial America is a question that probably admits of a lot of different answers. You can see Nirvana (and grunge in general) as representing the last dregs of the comedown from rock's utopian high in the Sixties, the point where the liberation mythology of the Baby Boomers fully gave way to the disengagement and damage of Generation X. It must have been disturbing, to say the least, for Cobain to realize what a compelling spectacle he made. Think of the terrible mass of rock clichés that swarmed around him: tortured rebel; weary hedonist; unwilling champion; pure soul lost in a sewer of disillusionment, dirty money and addiction. It didn't matter which (if any) of these templates were true, only that they could be stuck to him and sold—the bitter irony being that the alienation and rage in Nirvana that people found so powerfully resonant suited the system perfectly. It was all food for MTV. So however forcefully the music's sentiment was expressed there remained the inescapable suspicion that it was at heart an empty and secretly complicit performance, a protest that attained no distance from what it protested. It was as if a death knell had been rung for the possibility of rock as any kind of subversive or politically transformative form of art. Whatever you did, however desperately you meant to rebel, the system never ceased to profit.

But the content of Nirvana's particular story, as poignant as it is, isn't the main thing that's stuck with me. It was rather the possibility it illuminated: however grim the connotations, here was music that acted as a beacon, alchemizing people's taste into a kind of mass statement about the world they occupied. I'm not saying these sorts of thoughts were clear in my head when I was younger and getting into grunge. But I would like to think a premonition was already there, and that beyond the basic thrill of the music it was this that gave the experience its weight—the apprehension that I was part of some grand audience, that millions of other people cared about the same thing, had absorbed the same bleak spectacle, and that we could relate. So the impression it left was maybe just that of having been, in however small a way, part of a moment of collective history, or at least within touching distance of it. I'm wondering if it isn't just misplaced nostalgia that makes it so hard to locate the same feeling in music today.

S IMON REYNOLDS HAS spent over a quarter of a century writing about pop music for a living.* He began his career at the (now-defunct) London

---

* Note: what counts as "pop music" isn't clearly defined and needn't correspond to music that's actually popular. For the purposes of this essay I have a very catholic sense of the term in mind: pop as comprising roughly (but not exclusively) any sort of electrified, rhythm-heavy music from the last sixty years or so that includes some element of mass appeal (e.g. rock, disco, reggae, heavy metal, dance, hip-hop, electronica, etc.). It might be best to define pop music negatively—as not-jazz, not-classical, not-traditional—although inevitably those boundaries are themselves imprecise. Essentially, I'm trusting you to know the sort of thing I mean.

magazine *Melody Maker* in 1985. His first book, *Blissed Out: The Raptures of Rock* (1990), a collection of articles from the period, is a giddy celebration of late-Eighties underground rock and neo-psychedelia. In 1994 he moved to New York and has lived in the United States ever since, relocating to Los Angeles in 2010. He has co-authored a book about rock music and gender theory, *The Sex Revolts: Gender, Rebellion and Rock 'N' Roll* (1995), with his wife Joy Press, and written journalistic histories of the two most important phases of his life in terms of music. *Energy Flash* (1998) documented the ascent of rave in Britain during the Nineties (a truncated edition has been published in America as *Generation Ecstasy*) and *Rip It Up and Start Again: Post-Punk 1978-84* (2005) recounted the supercharged period that followed the rise and fall of punk rock. The latter is supported by a companion volume of interviews with musicians, *Totally Wired: Post-Punk Interviews and Overviews* (2009). Since 2002, Reynolds has maintained an informal blog, Blissblog, which operates as a fermenting lab and a fragmented running commentary on his ideas.

Retromania is Reynolds's seventh book. It begins from the premise that the last ten years in popular culture (but specifically pop music) have been fixated on the has-been and the already-done, while being conspicuously barren in terms of distinct, innovative content of their own. *Retromania* isn't a systematic study of retro culture so much as an overview of issues relating to this strange sense of ennui that's been a part of Western pop culture since (at least) the turn of the millennium. These topics include, but aren't limited to: the impact of the digital revolution on artistic creation and consumption; the death or decline of "modernist" ideology in popular culture; the history of pop-nostalgia; the undying allure of revivalism; and the role of the critic in the digital era. Many, if not all, of these subjects would warrant a book-length study of their own, and Reynolds doesn't arrive at a lot of firm conclusions—instead offering sketches, speculations and personal impressions of the *zeitgeist*.

The broad point, however, about the general backwardness of pop since the millennium seems eminently plausible, and to my mind even a cursory sense of the relevant history supports it. "The Nineties felt like this long, sustained ascent, what with the Internet and the info-tech boom, techno rave and its associated drugs," notes Reynolds. "But the 2000s turned out to be a plateau ... it seemed like nothing *momentous* had happened. Worse, it was a struggle to pinpoint what defined the era as a separate era musically." An intuitive test for this theory is supplied by the tech-philosopher Jaron Lanier in his excellent *You Are Not a Gadget* (2010). "Popular music created in the industrialized world in the decade from the late 1990s to the late 2000s doesn't have a distinct style," he writes, "that is, one that would provide an identity for the young people who grew up with it."

I have frequently gone through a conversational sequence along the following lines: Someone in his early twenties will tell me I don't know what I'm talking about, and then I'll challenge that person to play me some music that is characteristic of the late 2000s as opposed to the late 1990s. I'll ask him to play the tracks for his friends. So far, my theory has held: even true fans don't seem to be able to tell if an indie rock track or a dance mix is from 1998 or 2008, for instance.

As both Reynolds and Lanier acknowledge, it seems incredibly unlikely that *nothing* has been made in Western pop in the last ten years that couldn't have been made in some earlier decade. But compared to the quantum leaps in style that used to occur periodically (think about how far away rock 'n' roll is from acid house) there is a remarkable dearth of what might be called "macro-scale" innovation: cultural explosions such as hip-hop in the 1980s or rave in the 1990s—scenes that not only centered on formally innovative music, but which inspired whole ways of life and distinct subcultures among significant chunks of the population.

The flipside to this phenomenon, in Reynolds's words, is retromania itself: "the vastly increased presence in our lives of old pop culture: from the availability of back-catalogue records to YouTube's gigantic collective archive and the massive changes in music consumption engendered by playback devices like the iPod (which often functions like a personal 'oldies' radio station)." As well as being more available than ever, the history of pop is lionized through endless parades of reissues, retrospectives, comebacks and commemorative box sets, while classic rock and pop acts ossify into monuments and museum pieces (many of which, nonetheless, continue to tour and record). There "has never been a society in human history so obsessed with the cultural artifacts of *its own immediate past*. That is what distinguishes retro from antiquarianism or history: the fascination for fashions, fads, sounds and stars that occurred within living memory." Retro isn't a trend confined to pop music by any means, but Reynolds is right to say that its presence there is especially jarring given the premium that pop supposedly attaches to freshness and novelty. New acts come and go, but the churn of faces and songs occurs inside a kind of stasis, like a high street where the shops constantly change but the atmosphere is fixed. In one way new things appear all the time. But in another nothing ever happens.

T HE IDEA THAT we live in a nostalgia-soaked culture isn't new. Historical novels, costume dramas, throwback fashion and Hollywood remakes
are all big business and have been for some time. But pop makes an interesting synecdoche for culture at large because the prominence of old content and
styles exists in an environment that, in another respect, is one of unprecedented
wealth. Thanks to the digital revolution, more people have access to more music
than at any point in the past. Likewise, given the relative ease of modern production and distribution, it's plausible that more content is being brought into the
world year-on-year too. The precise causes of retromania are things Reynolds
speculates about without fixing on, but clearly he thinks the link between the
stall in pop innovation and the spread of digital technology is non-contingent—
which seems like a reasonable supposition, if only because it is hard to imagine
two such pronounced trends in the same field being unrelated.*

What's novel about retromania isn't the influence of the past on present
music (if that were the case, it would be nearly as old as pop itself) but rather
the depth and breadth of the phenomenon, the impression it creates of total
immersion and immutability. Bob Dylan aped Woody Guthrie, the Rolling
Stones stole from old bluesmen, etc.—but still something vividly distinct was
fashioned in the process. It's this sensation of movement from the inherited
to the unfamiliar that seems to have vanished. Pop is no longer premised on
forward motion. "I'm not claiming that all the retro music is disappointing,"
remarks Lanier. "But this is the first time since electrification that mainstream
youth culture in the industrialized world has cloaked itself primarily in nostalgic
styles." I grew up with the idea, for example, that part of what it was to belong
to a particular generation was having music that belonged to you, as opposed to
previous generations or generations yet to come. But as Lanier says, retro pop
seems utterly incapable of providing any distinct identity for the young people
who "own" it, because it has none (which perhaps helps to account for a relatively common complaint about modern pop, one that otherwise seems hard to

---

* In an interview with The A.V. Club, Reynolds commented: "You can date the beginning of
the non-appearance of [new musical] movements almost precisely to when the internet becomes
a major force in music culture. As soon as that really starts to take hold as being the major
means through which fans talk to each other and everything else that came with the internet,
it's almost from that point onwards that there've been no movements on the scale of hip-hop
and rave." Lanier offers more of a theory for this connection. The problem as he conceives it
is a combination of technological "lock-in" (MIDI, a tool invented in the Eighties to represent
musical notes in software, is now an almost universal and practically unavoidable component of
digital music technology—the trouble being that this confines digitized music to a certain range
of pre-established possibilities) and more generally the fact that digital aesthetic technology is
predisposed to fragmentation and copying, meaning that as digitization has spread so too has
derivative, "second-order" culture.

explain considering just how much different stuff there is to listen to—namely that it's flavorless, forgettable).

The extent of retro's hold over the cultural imagination is revealed by the very demographic you would expect it to have the least power over: the cutting-edge artistic class—i.e. "hipsterland, pop's equivalent to highbrow." As Reynolds observes, the "very people who you would once have expected to produce (as artists) or champion (as consumers) the non-traditional and the groundbreaking—*that's* the group who are most addicted to the past." *Retromania* points to a striking decline in "irony free" sci-fi imagery in pop compared to the Sixties or even to the Nineties. In the prevailing atmosphere it seems easier or somehow more legitimate for young artists to envision themselves as archaeologists rather than cosmonauts, the dominant modes being those of recycling, remixing and recombination—techniques that might well involve brilliant creativity, but are essentially parasitic.

During the course of a lengthy profile written for *The Wire* magazine on the Los Angeles independent record label Not Not Fun (run by husband and wife team Britt and Amanda Brown) Reynolds homes in on this point:

> Asked if they can delineate the sensibility of their generation, Britt and Amanda's thoughts converge with my own doubts. "I consider it to be post-creation," offers Amanda. "Pastiche. We're all now just *pulling* and *pulling* and *pulling*. Someone like Prince was thinking of people in the past, but it didn't feel as funnelled and as specific. We're a bit derivative, unfortunately, and it's not to our detriment always—but we are direct descendants and there are all these lineages. It's an interesting time for music because people aren't trying to create anything brand new." She points to [Not Not Fun] artist Umberto: "He's making music that sounds like Goblin, which you'll have heard of if you've watched old Argento movies. But he's one of the few people making that kind of music today. So that is the choice you make: you go for who is stepping a little bit outside of the box—the box being the demos we get sent everyday. But you can't say 'Umberto, he's so original.' Originality is not a thing anymore."

Reynolds is at pains to stress that it is hardly as if retro lacks charm or precludes good music from being made (the profile of Not Not Fun is very positive). Yet the impression lingers that something important has gone missing. "Given that I enjoy so many aspects of retro," Reynolds asks at the beginning of *Retromania*, "why do I still feel deep down that it is lame and shameful?" At least part of the answer is that for all its pleasures retro culture seems fundamentally tame. What troubles Reynolds about hipster-retroism isn't anything viscerally displeasing about the music or the type of person who makes it. It's more the awareness that the sort of lighthearted, cosmopolitan sensibility it suits also fits rather too well with other forms of safe, tasteful consumerism, "right next to distressed furniture, microbrew beer, artisanal cheese and vintage clothing." It feels like creativity without any existential urgency. "No longer art as an intervention in the battlefield of culture, but art as 'décor for life.'"

In an interview with *FACT* magazine in 2007, Reynolds remarked that his entire critical sensibility—from the more flamboyant prose of his early articles and essays (where he enthusiastically delved into concepts of blissful self-annihilation; *jouissance*; "re-mystification") to the mature phase of his writing—could be boiled down to a hunt for "intensity." That is: "The serious-as-your-life of aesthetic rapture, the seriousness of taking music and the discourse around it intensely seriously, reading a lot into music. Maybe to the point of mania or fanaticism." Reynolds is not the only one to have connected the dearth of innovation in pop with its "disintensification." In a piece for *n+1* reviewing the first fifteen years of the music website *Pitchfork*, Richard Beck equated the immobility of contemporary independent rock with its decline into an arena of complacent, cultural-capital driven fashions—a judgment that clearly echoes Reynolds's worries about underground music becoming a form of niche consumerism. Both arguments seem to interpret the lack of artistic evolution as a sign of impotence, specifically pop's powerlessness to effect change on the social or political level. The belief that music could invade—and remake—all things public and private is part of the primordial myth of rock. Since at least the Sixties, new art held out the promise of a new life, and reinvention on the personal level could be revolution on the social. "Confronted with performers as appealing and disturbing as Elvis Presley, the Beatles, or the Sex Pistols, with people who raise the possibility of living in a new way," Greil Marcus wrote, "some respond and some don't— and this, if only for a moment, becomes a primary social fact." Indeed, the idea that musical innovation bears a relationship to social upheaval goes back as far as Plato, whose *Republic* warns us that "the modes of music are never disturbed without unsettling the most fundamental political and social conventions."

From this angle, what retromania heralds isn't the death of pop as an area of creativity, but the demise of a certain type of (political) possibility. Genres of music that were once outlets for waves of discontented energy have been subdued and subsumed into the consumerist hegemony—rock, punk, hip-hop and the rest turned into competing leisure options rather than activities with any subversive potential. In the absence of new styles to take their place, pop petrifies as a social force.

REYNOLDS DESCRIBES HIS sensibility as a modernist one. The term "modernist" (like its relation, "postmodernist") struggles with competing and unsettled definitions. Nevertheless, one comparatively straightforward way of grasping *Retromania* is to see it as part of a family of Western cultural theory that takes a dim view of the shift from modernism to postmodernism in the arts—associating the former (speaking roughly) with creativity that involves some authentic political and/or ethical investment, and the latter with an aesthetic that takes art as a sort of fun but frivolous mode of play, wherein values of authenticity and commitment are relegated beneath those of diversity, irony and masquerade. Reynolds attributes his modernist ethos to the post-punk scene he immersed himself in as a teenager, the culture he subsequently chronicled in *Rip It Up and Start Again*—an assembly of artists united less by style than ideology, inspired by punk's destructive energy but "who saw 1977 not as a return to raw rock 'n' roll but as a chance to make a break with tradition ... who defined punk as an imperative to constant change." These were the years of PiL, Joy Division, Talking Heads, Pere Ubu, the Slits, Scritti Politti, Gang of Four, Devo and Wire, to name only a few. It was an era filled to the brim with (often comically grandiose) conceptual and aesthetic ambition. The music was "modernist," in Reynolds's sense, not only because it invented new styles and involved a conscious commitment to futurity, but because it seemed to demand a level of radical seriousness in its performance—the full-bore conviction that what was being done mattered, that it could change society or lives or both. Post-punk modernism, apart from being a rapturous thrill in itself ("As I recall it now, I *never* bought any old records. Why would you?"), became the radiant standard for pop for the rest of Reynolds's career. In *Retromania*, he reiterates:

> When I started taking more than a passing interest in pop, as a teenager in the post-punk seventies, I immediately ingested a strong dose of modernism: the belief that art has some kind of evolutionary destiny, a teleology that manifests itself through genius artists and masterpieces that are monuments to the future. It was there already in rock, thanks to The Beatles, psychedelia and progressive rock, but post-punk drastically amped up the belief in constant change and endless innovation. Although by the early eighties modernism was thoroughly eclipsed within art and architecture, and postmodernism was seeping into popular music, this spirit of modernist pop carried on through rave and the experimental fringe of rock. These surges of renewal served as a booster shot for me, reconfirming the modernist credo: art should constantly push forward into new territory, reacting against its own immediate predecessors in violent gestures of severance, jettisoning its superseded stages like a rocket shooting into space.

The import of post-punk (and later rave) for Reynolds is that it turned pop modernism into more than just a theory or an aesthetic preference. There it described a *bona fide* ethos for living, one which survived and prospered outside the ghettos of the art world. One almost has to think that the commitment these scenes inspired bore a direct relation to their sense of being historically unique, which raises an interesting question about the relationship between the vitality of an artistic movement and its sense of time. Modernist art as Reynolds sketches it—centered on the principle of answering and "surpassing" old culture—depends on the concept of historical continuity: a series of distinct artistic phases, each forming in reaction to their predecessors and, in turn, inspiring their own fresh opposition. This sort of modernism doesn't hang together without the idea of temporal succession, not only because it depicts a necessary antagonism between old art and new, but because it's premised on the idea of a deficient present that needs to be broken with in favor of tomorrow. Again, the dominant metaphor is of forward-motion: rushing ahead into the unknown, the New.

My generation can be said to straddle two eras: still in touch with the idea of historical succession in and through music, we arrived at maturity just as the digital revolution took hold and that sense of linearity and temporal definition started to dissolve. "Atemporal" is how Reynolds characterizes the contemporary pop environment—a zone at once engulfed by the debris of the past and yet eerily timeless. "If you are under the age of 25," he writes, "and have grown up with a relationship to music based around total access and the erosion of a sense of sounds belonging to a historical sequence, thinking about music in terms of development through time becomes alien and unrecoverable."* The term Reynolds coins for the feel of the last decade in pop is "hyper-stasis," meant to capture the sensation of velocity within closed loops, motion without travel; as if culture now formed an enormous, barely mappable totality within which all possibilities were already contained. For artists, history becomes more than just a burden; it becomes the complete enclosure within which their activity takes place, too huge to escape—perhaps too huge to even recognize as an enclosure. In all of this, the loss of contrast is a recurring motif: either temporally (now/then) or politically (us/them). It is even detectable in the redundancy of certain terms of art redolent of physical journeying (the idea of an *avant-garde* or of artistic "movements"—concepts made hollow if, creatively, there's nowhere to go).

Reynolds doesn't make explicit whether he thinks that, insofar as retromania represents the "defeat" of modernist ambitions in pop, it belongs under the umbrella of postmodernism, but it's an intuitive thought. "Postmodernism"

---

* This quote is from "Excess All Areas," a sister-essay to *Retromania* published in *The Wire* #328.

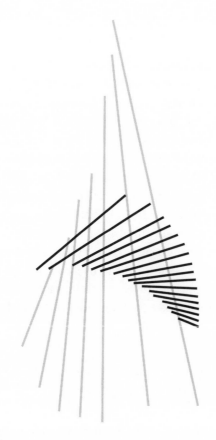

(like "modernism") can be used to describe both an artistic style and a historical situation ("the postmodern era"). Think about it in the latter sense and you see retromania in a freshly problematic light. If much of what Reynolds says amounts to hypothesizing a link between progressivism and artistic "intensity," what makes it troublesome as a prescriptive philosophy—as he must know—is that it isn't clear it makes sense to think of this as a matter of artistic will, as if someone could simply decide to be original or timely.*

D OES ANY OF this necessarily make pop less enjoyable? Reynolds never poses the question so directly. Near the end of *Retromania*, he admits that abandoning his modernist ideals would feel like "settling for less"—and that may be true insofar as "modernism" is simply being used as a byword for especially intense or committed forms of art. But in a way this is only to return to the problem just described, since the concern is whether modernist assumptions still have any application in a culture that appears to have fallen drastically out of sync with them. To put the matter slightly differently, the bedrock issue in *Retromania* is whether there's reason to believe that the prevalence of atemporal/post-historical pop actually diminishes the experience of music, even for kids whose expectations of it must be radically different from Reynolds's. And whatever the trouble might be, it is ridiculous to say that it's a question of there not being enough good songs to listen to or new records to discover. The sheer volume of music available makes it almost impossible to believe that anyone,

---

* Two terms that occur over and over in conversations about culture in the last decade are "post-historical" and "post-geographical." For example, Reynolds cites the concept of "Fifth World Music" as a possible name for the mash of transworld/time-hopping pop made using modern digital tools (the term itself is derivative, an exaggeration of Jon Hassell's concept of "Fourth World Music," which described a similarly omnivorous, if less generalized, style in the Eighties). It denotes an aesthetic of maximalist indeterminacy that perhaps comes closest to passing for a distinct strain in recent pop—a style that is really just the clearest manifestation of the dissolve-and-merge effects of the internet. But even if you were prepared to call this hyper-blend a genuinely unique form of modern pop, it is worth noting how it's defined by a *lack* of particulars, a blankness-at-heart. Indeed, the notion of "post-geographical" or "post-historical" categories of art remains in some essential ways hard to credit, since (surely) artists and audiences alike must still be located somewhere in time and space, no matter how far the internet allows their attention to travel. Like "postmodernism" itself, the concepts seem at once apt and rather empty. Certainly they indicate something real, but they're also principally words for non-states (ones "beyond" modernism, history, geography), curiously mute about what contemporary culture *is* in the positive sense. It's a linguistic failing that perhaps indicates something oddly void about the present—as if describing our moment in history required thoughts we are not quite capable of forming.

with a bit of effort, couldn't find enough material to like. The problem, such as it is, has to be something more subtle.

The way I've been putting it to myself is this: Is music today important or not? On the face of it, the question is absurd. In the most general sense, music seems like such an inarguable good—such a basic fusion of human instinct and achievement—that its goodness isn't something you can express properly with words. Nietzsche put it beautifully when he said that without music life would be "a mistake." How could it *not* be important? And yet I've had a feeling for several years now—the best way I can describe it is as a vague sense of cultural weightlessness, the impression that while there's an overwhelming amount of high-quality art out there to enjoy, there's also something terribly insubstantial about it, taken in sum. Or if not insubstantial exactly, then contained, settled, offering a type of pleasure that seems to be always and already conscious of its own limits. Pop is only a single case of this, but it's an exemplary one. It's as though some trick of perspective were at work: close up, the form is teeming and rich and apparently endlessly interesting, whereas as a whole it feels inconsequential, indistinct and strangely dull—a field of creativity disconnected from history, confused about what it can or ought to aspire to.

Whatever else, *Retromania* offers some evidence that this isn't just an ungrateful conceit. The problem it comes out of, I think, is a quintessentially modern one—namely, how much effort it takes to convince yourself that all the cultural paraphernalia decorating your life (the books read, films watched, paintings examined, fashions worn, etc.) aren't just diversions or toys. Slavoj Zizek once suggested that these days the term "culture" has become a floating signifier for "all those things we practice without really believing in them, without 'taking them seriously,'"—which is to say, not things (we feel in our heart of hearts) that exercise any genuine power over our lives, and hence not things that can ever quite avoid the stain of frivolity or purposelessness. Accordingly, the abiding problem in modern criticism is how to understand what it is for art to be "serious" or to be worthy of taking seriously (something Reynolds gestures at with his juxtaposition between music as "décor for life" and music as a source of living conviction). Pop is one of the best examples of this problem because of its ubiquity. Over and above the common sense point that people are less likely to invest emotionally in something they can have with minimal effort and at almost no cost, the saturation of waking life with pop (via television, radio, advertisements, the internet, iPods, ringtones, etc.) smothers it beneath the forces of familiarity, habit and banality. For someone like Reynolds, who's spent his life immersed in pop and its assortments, the question of how to justify all that vanished time will weigh heavier, but the basic anxiety can't be uncommon. What *does* all this stuff matter?

Retromania testifies to an unprecedented difficulty in constructing answers to that question—not a failure of enjoyment *per se*, but something more like a failure of expression, a breakdown in significance. As we've seen, the deluge of retro coincides with the decay of all sorts of old dialects (to do with opposition, identity, rebellion, change) that were essential to expressing what pop might stand for. These venerable ways of speaking no longer "fit" in the right manner. But instead of new exchanges coming to take their place we confront a widespread failure-to-impart. You can see this dynamic in microcosm in Reynolds's observation that the most dispiriting thing about retro-pop isn't that it belongs to the past but that its period sheen conceals a fundamental lack of attachment. This stuff doesn't really "belong" anywhere, being more like a pseudo-image of the past than an artifact with any real historical content (but, for that very reason, also something that isn't quite at home in the present). Likewise, the abstractions and dissolutions involved in the concepts of "post-historical" or "post-geographical" pop create serious obstacles to expression, seeming to herald the unsustainability of old conversations without promising the advent of fresh ones. All of this lends itself to a peculiar type of voicelessness—either because pop signifies much less than it used to or because what it now signifies is extremely difficult to talk about. Tellingly, Reynolds observes that the characteristic sign of modernist art is that it challenges critics to come up with new concepts and terminologies to describe it, whereas under retromania criticism is condemned to rehash old conversations or to drop into listless cycles of self-questioning. What *Retromania* is "about," at its core, is a radical loss of things to say. It is in that sense a work of critical mourning, of mourning *for* the work of criticism, and for a world in which it was self-evident that pop could absorb and reward the critic's attention.

But it would be a mistake to think of this as representing a problem only for a certain kind of writer. Criticism is, in the end, just the most refined and fully realized way of talking about art, which is to say that where critics have trouble finding things to say it tends to indicate a more common loss of voice. As such, thinking about how retromania affects pop criticism is a good way of thinking about how retromania affects you, because what it illustrates is the sense in which communication (or the possibility of communication) has been stifled, the general impoverishment of the conversation in and around pop music. This dynamic doesn't make it impossible to enjoy pop, or to be moved by it, or to attach deep personal significance to a piece of music, but nor does it leave those experiences untouched. Most obviously, pop's ability to act as a vehicle for collective expression and unity is drastically reduced. So whereas formerly the music you liked might give you access to a segment of history (Nirvana could be a source of collective identity as well as the latest manifestation in the

continuum of rock), more often today the music you like is simply the music you like. But an excess of privacy ultimately leads to the impression that what you do (or are) doesn't matter, and even intensely personal responses to art can lose something if they elude communication completely, insidiously feeding the sensation that these things you experience and value so centrally are somehow groundless or insignificant or lonely. The fear it summons is exactly what Zizek latched onto with his remark that "culture" stands for the things we do without really believing in them—that all of these pleasures meant to add excitement and definition to our existence are somehow failures, in reality serving only to protect an illusion of movement and color.

M Y IMPRESSION IS that a very large part of what distresses Reynolds when he talks about retro and the disintensification of pop is that, in the end, these developments mean that pop gives a person less to show for the passage of time. The diminishment of critical "voice" is one way in which this manifests itself, but hardly the only one. "Music is conventionally regarded as the soundtrack to a life," Reynolds notes; "the favorite song as a commemoration, a Proustian trigger that sets you adrift on memory bliss." For the majority of us, music is the art that most thoroughly and powerfully mediates our sense of the past—both historically (the most efficient way of evoking period mood is through music) and personally. Music is a memory-weave: a trigger and a pathway to bygone time. And yet one of the most disconcerting things about retromania is that pop, the dominant music of our society, no longer conveys the movement of time in the same way. Rather than progressing through distinct periodic shifts, hyper-static culture presents an endless, homogenous churn of everything there ever was. So while personal memory and pop might still entwine, in a sense the memories record less, because they're tied to a medium that doesn't mark change. Perhaps the most straightforward reading of the various critical banners Reynolds unfurls (in favor of intensity, potency, commitment) is that they embody a desire to disrupt the quotidian, to not let time slip away unmarked or uncolored. Which is another reason why retro feels so fundamentally shameful, even repellent: because it suppresses pop's capacity to demark and define experience. The anguish *Retromania* betrays is the anguish of memory loss or oblivion—the fear of time (our life) disappearing without a trace.

As he finishes, Reynolds reaffirms his belief that pop is still capable of the shocks it once supplied. His final line is a declaration of optimism: "I still believe the future is out there." But it is extremely hard to know what to make of this. How can you maintain a modernist imperative to change in a situation in which change feels unimaginable? What sort of programmatic response could be given to retromania if, as it seems, the phenomenon is bound up with enormous technological and cultural shifts that couldn't be undone even if we wished them to be? The future Reynolds believes in seems to be just another abstraction—"post-now," inconceivable in its specifics.

But then maybe the point is just to hold on to the ideal, even in the abstract. Perhaps this is all *Retromania* can plausibly offer: a defense against a certain type of fatalism, which doubles as an exercise in remembering. Pop really did do these things: possessed, inspired, ignited and transformed on a mass scale. To maintain a belief in the (artistic) future—even just as an empty category—is a means of preserving the memory of desire, of reminding oneself what pop could be, because it once was. The principle then is not to reverse time but to make it reappear, as a past that had substance and a tomorrow with possibility. To resist, in other words, retro's anaesthetic.

The viability of this mission is an open question and the impasses it seems to run into are formidable. Nonetheless it has the virtue of illuminating something valuable, which is simply the importance of not mistaking what's apparent now for what's possible. That may appear to be rather a thin substitute for the brilliant bursts of modernist enthusiasm Reynolds evokes. Yet insofar as that old excitement still holds an allure for us today, surely a huge part of the reason is that such music took itself to be more than just art; that it seemed to *require* itself to be more in order to qualify as art at all. (Compare that to the malaise of "culture" in Zizek's sense: art that lacks affect precisely because we can't see it as anything else.) If there is a route through the conceptual deadlock with which *Retromania* concludes, it may well be that this is the kind of question we should ask: In what ways can we *imagine* music—or any art—exceeding itself today? What is so imposing is the sense one sometimes has that we would need to re-equip or retrain our imaginations before we could answer.

Pete Souza, *Untitled*, 2009

SOCIALISM WE CAN BELIEVE IN

(PART I)

by Jonny Thakkar

Forsooth, brethren, fellowship is heaven, and lack of fellowship is hell: fellowship is life, and lack of fellowship is death: and the deeds that ye do upon the earth, it is for fellowship's sake that ye do them, and the life that is in it, that shall live on and on for ever, and each one of you part of it, while many a man's life upon the earth from the earth shall wane. Therefore I bid you not dwell in hell but in heaven, or while ye must, upon earth, which is a part of heaven, and forsooth no foul part.

WILLIAM MORRIS, *A DREAM OF JOHN BALL*

66 CHANGE WILL NOT come if we wait for some other person or some other time. We are the ones we've been waiting for. We are the change that we seek." Four years on, the heady idealism of 2008 makes me cringe like a purple passage in a teenage diary, like an old love letter excavated from a dusty pile. In some respects the frustration of that first term has been a uniquely American story: with its two houses, both alike in dignity, Congress will always produce legislation that satisfies no one in particular, and America's non-stop election calendar will inevitably encourage centrism. But the path that leads a Leftist from "Change We Can Believe In" to "Better The Devil You Know" has become familiar throughout the West. To Brits like myself, for instance, the Obama cycle feels like a Hollywood remake of Tony Blair's premiership (1997 slogan: "Things Can Only Get Better"), which itself appeared in theaters alongside the French version—more conversation, less drama—starring Lionel Jospin (1997 slogan: "Let's Change The Future"). And all three remind you of Bill Clinton.

In each case the activist "base" seems to go through the same emotional cycle:

(1) *anger* at right-wing government precedes

(2) *hope* in a new Left and

(3) *election* of a new government;

(4) *disgust* at that government's compromises gives way to

(5) *protest* at betrayals, leading to

(6) *refusal* to vote which produces

(1) *anger* at right-wing government.

At the time of writing, Britain has returned to (1) under David Cameron, although there are hints of (2); France is between (3) and (4) with François Hollande; and the U.S. has just decided (narrowly) not to convert (5) into (6) and hence (1). The most interesting phase is clearly (4): disgust at compromise. Why should the base find compromise *disgusting*? Everyone knows you can't always get what you want—that may be disappointing, but it does not, on the face of it, seem disgusting. Yet that is precisely the point. What offends Leftists is the suspicion that their leaders are not actually *compromising* but *triangulating*. Compromise is something you do when you know your desired destination; triangulation, by contrast, is just negotiating to stay in power.

Yet it's not as if the base itself has any kind of articulated vision of the good society. Take last year's Occupy protests in America and beyond. "We are winning," they cried. But what exactly were they trying to win? Whereas the Tea Party placed candidates into elected office, and forced others to bend to its will by orchestrating debates, rallies and pledges, Occupy renounced such ambitions from the start. Policies and politics are for dupes, it seemed to sneer: the old world is beyond saving. The idea, its leaders proclaimed, was to model a new direct democracy in which there are no leaders. But if the movement was itself the message, the message was hardly appealing: anyone who has endured student government knows that when everyone talks, nothing gets decided. And this indecision seemed all too convenient, as many pointed out, since it allowed the protesters to wash their hands of the responsibility that comes with concrete commitments.

It may have been unfair to expect detailed policies from the Occupiers. But the real critique was harder to answer: What, the critics asked, is your vision of the good life? And not just the good life in general, but the good life for *us*, here and now in the twenty-first century West? How does the model of tent-dwelling anarcho-democrats debating long into the night relate to the problem of contemporary inequality? It's all well and good attacking corruption and cronyism, but inequality is also a function of globalization, which turns first-world countries into service economies that reward the educated and screw the rest. Viewed in this light, Occupy's central slogan—"We are the 99%"—was as facile as they come; the editor of *The Occupy Handbook* actually bragged that "Occupy Wall Street has the rare distinction of being a protest movement that even the objects of its attack can find little fault with." Like the Harvard lawyer at whose feet many of its participants had knelt three years earlier, Occupy managed to wrap itself in the aura of Che Guevara while offending nobody. *We are the ones we've been waiting for.*

Obama and Occupy seem to represent the exhaustion of the Western Left in general. Yet the mood of cynicism, wry and weary, to which I, like so many, presently find myself tempted, can be as blinding as the most dizzying optimism. To dismiss 2008 as mere showbiz, or the Occupy movement as mere self-righteous escapism, would be to ignore the significance of the springs from which they drew: widespread dissatisfaction, even despair, at the status quo; and a yearning, however inarticulate or inchoate, for fundamental transformation. That this yearning has so readily found expression in vacuities points to its strength, not its weakness; if it is capable of sustaining us in empty illusions, at least for a time, that only goes to show how desperately we crave escape from the fetters of contemporary politics. And it is notable that in promising us relief, Obama and Occupy both pointed to the same kind of destination: setting their faces against self-seeking individualism, they spoke to us as individuals in search of self-transcendence. They spoke, that is, to our desire for community without collectivism, for a community forged from the ground up, by us ourselves, in a spirit of what the French Revolutionaries called "fraternity." *We are the change that we seek.*

The problem was that neither Obama nor Occupy was able to give the idea of fraternity any real substance. For Obama, it seemed to imply campaign contributions; for Occupy, endless discussions. Neither could connect it to the imperatives of our changing economic climate or to the day-to-day decisions and actions that together constitute society. This, not their idealism, was their failing. If fraternity is to be more than a utopian fantasy or a pious palliative, it will need to find expression in an ethic that can be lived out in everyday life, in institutions that are within our grasp, in a vision of a future radically better than the present yet recognizably rooted in its conditions.

A MONG THE MANY paradoxes of contemporary politics is the fact that the concept of fraternity now finds its home on the Right, not the Left— at least ostensibly. The Right is a broad church, if a church it is, and between the neoliberals and the theocrats sit the "civic" conservatives, represented by intellectuals like Yuval Levin and David Brooks in America, and Phillip Blond, Jesse Norman and David Willetts in Britain. Civic conservatism shares neoliberalism's suspicion of collectivist welfare but rejects its absolute faith in markets; it holds that social services are best provided neither by the state nor by corporations, but by the "little platoons" and "local associations" through which citizens help one another in a spirit of fraternity and fellowship.

It's easy to dismiss civic conservatism as mere lipstick on the neoliberal pig. Certainly there is more than a whiff of comedy in the titles under which it has labored: "compassionate conservatism" in the case of George W. Bush, a man whose own compassion tended to be well hidden, shall we say, behind his stiff upper cheek; and "Big Society" in the case of David Cameron, who, having coined an empty phrase, felt the need to commission academics to decipher its "difficult to pin down" values. Given that the centerpiece of civic conservatism—the idea of freeing civil society from the state—coincides rather neatly with the need to cut government budgets, many have concluded that it is, as the Archbishop of Canterbury put it, "aspirational waffle designed to conceal a deeply damaging withdrawal of the state from its responsibilities to the most vulnerable." And it does seem to be private companies that increasingly run prisons, parks and even orphanages, rather than the charities and churches that get highlighted in the prospectus.

But accusations of bad faith are more emotionally gratifying than productive. For the idea of reviving an ethic of locally rooted public service actually expresses our yearning for fraternity rather well. As the "Red Tory" policy guru Phillip Blond puts it, the past few decades have seen Right and Left conspire to shift power away from local communities. To reverse the shift towards big business and the big state would be to create a big society. Communities must be given more legislative powers to shape their neighborhoods; parent-run schools, mutual insurance funds and cooperative ventures must be encouraged; and citizens must engage in community service. From the perspective of fraternity— community without collectivism—that all sounds exceedingly noble. And that only makes its failings more interesting. For the problem with civic conservatism is at root intellectual rather than moral—as will become clear if we consider another of Cameron's grand slogans.

When Cameron first called Britain a "Broken Society," in a 2009 speech, it seemed a little hysterical. As the *Economist* lost no time in pointing out, crime had dropped 45 percent since 1995; the number of teenage mothers had halved since 1969; the divorce rate was the lowest since 1979; and in the previous five years there had been a fall in drug abuse. But when rioting befell Britain the summer before last, Cameron seemed vindicated. What began as a protest against police brutality in one of London's poorest districts somehow snowballed into a seemingly senseless spree of theft and vandalism across the country: 3,443 crimes were committed in less than a week, resulting in five deaths and damage worth £200 million. In Cameron's words, echoing many a right-wing jeremiad, this destructive frenzy was simply the logical conclusion of the "slow-motion moral collapse that has taken place in parts of [the U.K.] these past few generations." Round up the usual suspects, he seemed to say—welfare, godlessness and the Sixties can step to the front.

Cameron has never addressed the concepts of Big Society and Broken Society in the same speech, it would appear—which is just as well, since they stand in flat contradiction. The central idea of the Big Society is that if we would only remove state interference then local non-profits would be able to take their rightful place in providing services. This presumes that the only thing preventing a vibrant array of volunteer associations from springing up all around us is the long shadow of the state. Yet if society is in fact *broken*, as Cameron suggests, then this premise will surely be false.

Perhaps Cameron means to imply that Broken and Big apply to different segments of society, with the well-adjusted "silent majority" sweeping up after the underclasses. This is of course an appealing thought for the majority, as many Western politicians have realized; Cameron's "Broken Society" slogan is itself borrowed from Jacques Chirac's 1995 campaign theme of "*la fracture sociale*," and Chirac's successor Nicolas Sarkozy came to power on the back of his 2005 denunciation of kids from the Parisian *banlieus* as "scum." But comforting as this picture may be, it flatters the majority. For if Western societies are indeed fractured along moral lines—if, that is, their underclasses seem to act as if they have no stake in the perpetuation of social norms—this fracture only expresses a deeper dysfunction, a "moral collapse," to use Cameron's expression, that is scarcely limited to one particular class.

Consider the riots. When the BBC asked two boys in Manchester why they were looting, one responded: "Why are you going to miss the opportunity to get free stuff that's worth loads of money?" Notice what the boy does not say: "I just joined in," for instance, or "I fancied some new shoes." Instead he offers a normative argument: anyone in his right mind would have done as I did. And the argument is logically sound. His premise is that of economic man: get as much as you can for as little cost as possible. In normal circumstances, the threat of punishment renders petty crime unprofitable, but in extraordinary times the costs and benefits shift. And if the expected return from theft—probable gain

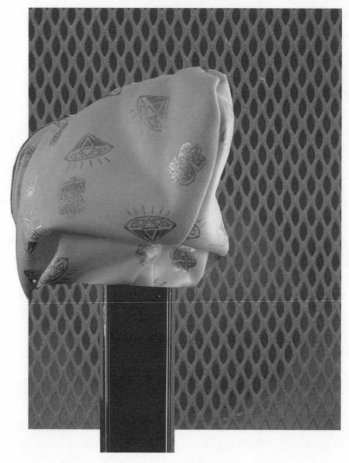

Geof Oppenheimer, *Chicago*, 2010

multiplied by probable cost—rises above zero, and no better opportunities present themselves, not to participate would be positively irrational.

This reasoning may be shocking, but it is hardly unfamiliar. Nor is it limited to one particular class—if anything, it is more common at the top than at the bottom. As the *Daily Telegraph* columnist Peter Oborne pointed out, in recent years Britain has seen bankers demand government handouts while awarding themselves colossal bonuses, politicians abuse parliamentary expenses for private gain, journalists hack the phones of celebrities and murder victims, and police accept payments from journalists. These crimes all share a basic structure with the boy's looting (and welfare scamming, for that matter): the gains were obvious, punishment seemed unlikely, and the victims were too distant to create what economic man would term "psychological costs," such as feelings of sympathy or guilt. In these circumstances—as when you come upon a wallet in a deserted street—only habit and shame can counteract self-interest. Perhaps self-interest simply overwhelmed them in battle. But an alternative explanation is that maximizing our own welfare at the expense of the community is no longer shameful—that it has, in fact, become a habit.

This might seem histrionic. Humans have always been self-interested, and every society has its monsters. Oborne himself tried to pin the blame on the monsters, especially those who set an example from the top of society, claiming that most people "continue to believe in honesty, decency, hard work, and putting back into society as much as they take out." But the prevailing ethos of a society manifests itself above all in what it considers shameful, since it is through developing a sense of shame that we learn to regulate our own behavior. And the evidence suggests that most Britons no longer consider self-seeking to be shameful, as one of Oborne's own observations shows:

> A few weeks ago, I noticed an item in a newspaper saying that the business tycoon Sir Richard Branson was thinking of moving his headquarters to Switzerland. This move was represented as a potential blow to the Chancellor of the Exchequer, George Osborne, because it meant less tax revenue. I couldn't help thinking that in a sane and decent world such a move would be a blow to Sir Richard, not the Chancellor. People would note that a prominent and wealthy businessman was avoiding British tax and think less of him. Instead, he has a knighthood and is widely feted.

The point is not that Branson has no sense of shame—his whole career, replete with self-promoting stunts such as driving a Sherman Tank down New York's Fifth Avenue to promote Virgin Cola, suggests a man who cares very deeply about his image. The point is rather that Britons do not shame him. If Britain is indeed suffering from a "moral collapse," as Cameron thinks, then the inability to find antisocial behavior shameful is at the root of it. Far from being on the margins of British society, the boy who could see no rational reason not to loot had only too firm a grasp on its dominant ethos.

And this ethos makes a mockery of civic conservatism. Cameron chose "Big Society" as a slogan because it allowed him to distance himself from Margaret Thatcher, who had infamously declared that "there is no such thing as society." In Cameron's view, there *is* such a thing as society, only buried beneath the stifling superstructure of the state; freed from the shackles of bureaucracy, civic-minded volunteers will inevitably spring up from every crack and crevice to usher in a golden age of civic-mindedness. But if a country's dominant ethos is egoistic—if antisocial behavior is no longer shameful—then this golden age is at best unlikely. And if an army of volunteers should *not* come forth once we have dismantled the state, there will be no option but to call in the for-profit contractors. In the final analysis, then, the Big Society is, as George Eaton pointed out in the *New Statesman*, no less utopian than Engels' infamous assertion that the state would eventually "wither away" under communism.

To change an ethos you need to change habits. Habits are the basic substance of moral life: they are the medium through which our values are translated daily, unthinkingly, into action; but they are also the medium through which our actions are translated, over the months and years, into values. If we spend our days looking out only for ourselves, trying to get as much as we can for as little cost as possible, are we really going to spend our nights volunteering at the soup kitchen? If fraternity is to be more than a campaign theme, an idle fantasy or a cynical ploy, it must be allowed to shape our day-to-day lives—and especially our day-to-day *work*. And with this in mind it is time to rethink an ideal whose very name is apt to make civic conservatives squirm.

S OMETIMES WE LOSE a concept without noticing. We carry on saying the words, but the life has gone out of them; shorn of the power to orient or inform, they serve only to mystify. Such is the fate, in the twenty-first century, of "socialism." In the United States it has become a term of abuse; elsewhere it is simply an abused term. Any attempt to reduce inequality can now be called socialist, it seems—from Barack Obama's plan to secure new customers for private insurance companies to Tony Blair's idea of unleashing the financial sector to pay for growth in public services. Of course everyone knew Blair was no socialist, whatever he claimed. And even the most rabid libertarian must be aware, deep down, that a President who calls the free market "the greatest force for economic progress in human history" is no socialist. But when it comes to someone like the new French president, François Hollande, leader of the *Parti Socialiste*, few would now object to the label. Hollande, reports the *New York Times*, "is vowing to impose a 75 percent tax on the portion of anyone's income above a million euros ($1.24 million) a year." This is the stuff of Occupy Wall Street's wettest dreams. But that does not, in and of itself, make it socialism.

To some extent the name is irrelevant: the important thing is to keep our concepts clear. But historically the name "socialism" has generally been used to describe a theory of *production* rather than a theory of *distribution*. In its most common form, it referred to the idea that the "means of production" ought to be brought under democratic control. The only time that Britain had an unequivocally socialist government, for instance, between 1946 and 1951, it nationalized the most important industries—coal, electricity, cable and wireless, rail, transport, gas, iron and steel—and created a state-run healthcare system. The hope was that collective ends would be better served if economic production were consciously regulated and controlled. This emphasis on the common good sprang from an egalitarian outlook, of course, and it typically involved the notion of redistribution, but those features were shared with left-liberalism. What distinguished socialism was its vision of an economy organized around service rather than profit.

If we have lost the concept of socialism, it is because we no longer consider it a genuine possibility. For although the notion that Eskimos have umpteen words for snow is now known to be a myth, it still expresses an important truth: we tend to make conceptual distinctions only when they seem useful. Europeans have often been struck by the way Americans equate the Left with liberalism; but since liberal is more or less as far left as anyone has ever gone in mainstream American politics, at least since Eugene Debs won 6 percent of the vote in the 1912 presidential election, there has never been any need to distinguish the two.* If the term socialist had been used to refer to liberals in mid-century Europe, in contrast, people would have needed a new term to describe the real socialists. For all the differences in their modes of self-understanding and self-presentation, Europe and America are now drawing closer politically. Socialism is now as dead in Europe as it is in America.

---

* Milwaukee did have socialist mayors in the periods 1910-12, 1916-40 and 1948-1960; and Bernie Sanders, now Senator for Vermont, is a self-described socialist. The question of why socialism has had so little impact in America has been subject to academic debate ever since Werner Sombart's 1906 tract, *Why is there No Socialism in the United States?* Possible causes include America's overwhelmingly rural geography; its federal constitution; racial divisions within the working class; and a pervasive spirit of individualism.

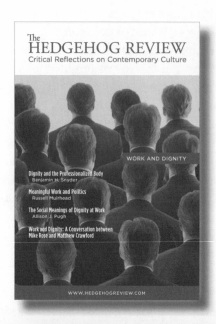

Socialists had often argued that collective ownership would produce efficiency gains: just as work in a factory is coordinated by a manager, rather than by an internal market, so whole industries could be administered rationally if freed from the dictates of the market. But this proved false. The real analogy, it turned out, was with the inefficiency of corporations freed from the pressures of competition: just as private monopolies grow bloated and fail to serve their customers, so do state monopolies. Those who ran state monopolies may have thought of themselves as public servants, but their good intentions were not enough. As Friedrich Hayek pointed out, they were simply too distant from conditions on the ground to allocate productive resources effectively.*

While the failures of nationalization can be overstated, they were nevertheless real. There were early successes: life expectancy rose, for instance, as did literacy and social mobility; gone forever were the brutal excesses of nineteenth-century Manchester, with its poverty, its disease, its wretched child labor. But by thinking of state ownership as *the* means to a fraternal society, socialists fell into treating it as an end in itself. They became *statists*. And since it will never be easy to discern the true face of brotherhood in the cold expression of a bureaucrat, the administrative state came to seem directly opposed to the realm of human association and mutuality. It was thus declared unwieldy and inhuman, a bloated monster that created dependency and suffocated local initiative. The logical response seemed to be privatization. And so, in one of history's little ironies, the idea of using public policy to engender fraternity became the political property of the Right.

At the same time, and largely as a result, the range of respectable economic thought narrowed considerably. Back when socialism seemed like a real possibility, the third way between it and laissez-faire liberalism was Keynesian liberalism. Keynesian liberalism shared socialism's aspiration to ensure full employment and the alleviation of poverty, but it also shared classical liberalism's skepticism concerning public ownership: all other things being equal, free markets were to be preferred. With socialism out of the picture, what had previously been the center now became the Left—or, to put it another way, the space of political possibility contracted. The dearth of compelling new ideas coming out of the endless discussions at Zuccotti Park bears witness to this contraction. We read Marx for the diagnosis, not the cure; Badiou and Zizek give us little more than

---

* In actual fact, socialist theorists had often been aware of this potential pitfall, but their proposed solution, which was usually some form of local democratic feedback, was impractical or at least ineffective—especially as compared to market prices, which aggregate information about consumer needs almost instantaneously.

R.H. Tawney

the frisson of a radicalism beyond comprehension; for actual policies, we can't think much beyond Paul Krugman.

But perhaps we need to rethink socialism. For what differentiates socialism from both left-liberalism and civic conservatism is, at bottom, its focus on the character of *work*, the day-to-day labor by which we produce both the world around us and, in the end, ourselves. And in and of itself this entails nothing about the *state*. Once socialism is distinguished from statism, it can also be liberated from it, both practically and theoretically. If we can find a non-statist mold into which to cast the core ideal of socialism, it might be possible for us to forge a politics of fraternity that is transformative without being utopian. And in this respect, I believe, our best guide might turn out to be a theorist described by Hayek himself as "a very wise man" and "a sort of socialist saint"—the inimitable R. H. Tawney (1880-1962).

T AWNEY WAS AN extraordinary character by any standard. Hugh Gaitskell, the former leader of the Labour Party, called him "the best man I have ever known"; *The Times* wrote that "no man alive has put more people into his spiritual and intellectual debt"; and his biographer Ross Terrill recounts that some claimed to have been converted to Christianity just by "the example of [his] humility, serenity and sense of ultimate things." Whereas many Leftist intellectuals stay aloof from the proletarians whose interests they claim to represent, or else content themselves with meaningless gestures of self-disavowal—a New York-based literary journal recently urged its readers to shred their college diplomas in solidarity with the masses—Tawney, still feeling his way into the nascent discipline of economic history after graduating from Oxford, decided to *serve* the proletariat, crisscrossing northern England every weekend to hold classes at trade unions and workers' institutes, debating the principles and practices of industrialism with weavers, potters and miners, and grading as many as 58 essays per week.

This life was shattered when the Great War erupted in 1914. Tawney enlisted straight away rather than waiting to be called up, turning down the class-based privilege of an officer's commission. This gesture proved to be of some importance: shot on the first day of the Somme in 1916, he was left lying on the battlefield for two days and then denied the care reserved for officers. When the Bishop of Oxford paid a concerned visit to the field hospital, the matron scolded her charge: "Why didn't you *tell* us you were a *gentleman?*" Nor did humility desert him even as he became one of the doyens of the Labour Party after the war. Teaching at the London School of Economics, Tawney once became so absorbed in his lecture that he placed his still-burning pipe into the pocket of his tweed jacket, which duly caught fire. Smoke billowing around him, his students looking on in silent consternation, he finally became aware of the fire, looked down, and calmly remarked: "I see I burn prematurely."

Tawney had friends in high places as well as low. On his first day at Rugby, one of England's most famous boarding schools, he met William Temple, who was not only the son of the Archbishop of Canterbury but himself went on to occupy the post during the Second World War. At Balliol College, Oxford, he fell in with the economist William Beveridge, later *Sir* William Beveridge, whose sister he married. Both friends later played crucial roles in the foundation of the postwar welfare state: Temple's best-selling *Christianity and the Social Order* (1942), published in his first year as Archbishop, developed the moral case; and Beveridge's seminal reports *Social Insurance and Allied Services* (1942) and *Full Employment in a Free Society* (1944) provided the blueprint. And in many ways these documents reflected the driving concerns of Tawney's own work.

Tawney is probably most famous for *Equality* (1931), in which he argued for an idea that remains radical to this day, if taken seriously: equality of opportunity. Nowadays everyone claims to believe in this ideal, Right and Left, yet few are willing to follow through on what it obviously entails. For without a certain measure of equality of outcome, one generation's equality of opportunity will be the next generation's class privilege. Given how alien the impassable hierarchies of Edwardian England now seem to us, Tawney's critique of his contemporaries remains surprisingly—and painfully—resonant:

> Most social systems need a lightning conductor. The formula which supplies it to our own is equality of opportunity. The conception is one to which homage is paid today by all, including those who resist most strenuously attempts to apply it. But the rhetorical tribute which it receives appears sometimes to be paid on the understanding that it shall be content with ceremonial honours. It retains its throne, on condition that it refrains from meddling with the profitable business of the factory and market-place. Its credit is good, as long as it does not venture to cash its cheques. Like other respectable principles, it is encouraged to reign, provided that it does not attempt to rule.*

---

* In the face of John Boehner-style success stories, whereby the successful rise of one member of the working class is held as an example to the rest, Tawney was simply sardonic: "It is possible that intelligent tadpoles reconcile themselves to the inconveniences of their position, by reflecting that, though most of them will live and die as tadpoles and nothing more, the more fortunate of their species will one day shed their tails, distend their mouths and stomachs, hop nimbly on to

It is hard to overestimate the influence of *Equality* on the British Left. So popular that in twenty-one years it went through four editions, its arguments effectively laid the groundwork for the welfare state created by Beveridge and company a decade later. "What is important," Tawney had written, "is not that all men should receive the same pecuniary income. It is that the surplus resources of society should be so husbanded and applied that it is a matter of minor significance whether they should receive it or not." The postwar welfare state expressed this principle in law: a couple would be given a pension that would allow them to grow old in dignity no matter how rich they or their children had become; a worker who went blind would receive disability compensation rather than being forced to beg from his neighbors; boys and girls would be educated to their full humanity regardless of the wealth or wisdom of their parents. The rich would help the poor not out of charity, with all the resentment and hypocrisy that can entail, but out of citizenly fellowship.

Yet the headline arguments of *Equality* were as congenial to left-liberals like Beveridge and John Rawls as they were to socialists. What made the book distinctively *socialist* were the sections that recapitulated Tawney's earlier works, which had focused on the nature of *production*. In *The Acquisitive Society* (1920), Tawney argued for a "functional society," in which work is organized towards the common good, as against an "acquisitive society," in which individuals work only for their own enrichment. During the war, a spirit of national unity had challenged the individualistic presuppositions of classical liberalism, and Tawney saw no reason why this ought not to be continued. In a 1918 essay, he had put this in the starkest terms:

> The right principle for the community to follow is simple, though its application may be complex. Though industrial reform cannot be imposed by the state, the state can, at least, emphasize the principle that industry and trade are a form of public service, and that the man who in time of peace plays on public necessities to amass a fortune—the monopolist, or the speculator who corners the market, or the urban landlord who grows rich by other men's industry—is morally on a par with the merchant or manufacturer who holds his countrymen to ransom in time of war.*

---

dry land, and croak addresses to their former friends on the virtues by means of which tadpoles of character and capacity can rise to be frogs. This conception of society may be described, perhaps, as the Tadpole Philosophy, since the consolation which it offers for social evils consists in the statement that exceptional individuals can succeed in evading them."

* One might think of this as one of the broader implications of Arthur Miller's 1947 play *All My Sons*; Miller was of course a socialist.

An industrialist who considered himself a public servant would, Tawney argued in that essay, offer the community the best service he could; he would charge the lowest price compatible with adequate payment for himself and his colleagues; he would redirect any surplus earnings back to the community; and if he provided no service he would demand no payment. The state would encourage this ethic by requiring him to publish a complete account of his costs and his profits, so that workers and customers could check if wages and prices were fair. But publicity, he conceded, was "no more than an antiseptic." What was needed was a cure.

The best-known argument in *The Acquisitive Society* concerns ownership. In a functional society, Tawney wrote—i.e. one in which every worker conceived of himself as a public servant—citizens would not consider property rights to be absolute or unequivocal; insofar as private ownership got in the way of service, it would be curtailed. If this sounds like the kind of revolutionary communism that gets people digging holes in their gardens and raising their mattresses by a few inches, Tawney insisted that it was quite the opposite: "If by property is meant the personal possessions which the word suggests to nine-tenths of the population, the object of Socialists is not to undermine property, but to protect and increase it." He wasn't thinking of ordinary household property, but of cases like coal deposits and capital inheritances. Suppose coal is discovered under your land. Why should it be thought of as *yours*? Why should you receive royalties for ever after, regardless of whether you perform any kind of service?

> The real analogy to many kinds of modern property is not the simple property of the small landowner or the craftsman, still less the household goods and dear domestic amenities, which is what the word suggests to the guileless minds of clerks and shopkeepers, and which stampede them into displaying the ferocity of terrified sheep when the cry is raised that "Property" is threatened. It is the feudal dues which robbed the French peasant of part of his produce till the Revolution abolished them. How do royalties differ from *quintaines* and *lods et ventes*?

This wasn't just a debating point. In 1919, Tawney served on a government commission on the future of the mining industry. Meeting various proprietors, he began to marvel at "the alchemy by which a gentleman who has never seen a coal mine distils the contents of that place of gloom into elegant chambers in London and a house in the country." In response to such functionless property rights, the commission concluded that the mines should be nationalized. Twenty-six years later, as part of the sweeping socialist agenda of the post-war Labour government, their proposal was finally enacted.

But what makes Tawney important today is not so much the fact that he advocated nationalization as *how* he advocated it. He always insisted that nationalization was a means, not an end; if it proved counterproductive, it should be jettisoned. And even if it were necessary, he thought, it could never be sufficient. Many socialists seemed to think that fraternity could be achieved from the top down, just through making industries accountable to elected politicians. But on Tawney's view nationalization would never produce fellowship if it took the responsibility for service away from workers themselves, denying them the freedom to exercise their own intellectual and creative capacities, and preventing them from transcending the acquisitive ethos for themselves. "However the socialist ideal may be expressed," Tawney insisted late in life, "few things could be more remote from it than a herd of tame animals with wise rulers in command."

What was needed, Tawney thought, was for *every* worker to conceive of himself as a public servant. This demand was above all ethical. But it wasn't simply pious utopianism, like the demand for politics without malice or stability without coercion. Tawney wanted to engender ethical change by institutional means, building on a resource already available in his society: the notion of a *profession*. Tawney defined a profession as "a trade which is organized, incompletely, no doubt, but genuinely, for the performance of a [social] function." Examples include medicine, teaching, law and the military, trades all governed by associations which prohibit conduct benefitting the individual worker at the expense of the community he is supposed to be serving.

> So, if they are doctors, they recognize that there are certain kinds of conduct which cannot be practiced, however large the fee offered for them, because they are unprofessional; if scholars and teachers, that it is wrong to make money by deliberately deceiving the public, as is done by makers of patent medicines, however much the public may clamor to be deceived; if judges or public servants, that they may not increase their incomes by selling justice for money; if soldiers, that the service comes first, and their private inclinations, even the reasonable preference of life to death, second.

In other words, professional associations are institutions that both foster and enforce an ethos of public service or professionalism. They are *self*-coercive: although answerable to the state at some level, they are constituted and regulated by workers themselves. As such they point to the possibility of instituting labor-based fraternity without resorting to either high-minded utopianism or oppressive collectivism. They point, in short, to a socialism we can believe in.

"WE ARE THE change that we seek," preached Barack Obama in 2008—
and he touched something in us, something that seemed both real and
utterly beyond grasp. In the years that followed, our rage was as much at our
own vagueness as it was at Obama's; when Occupy Wall Street revived the idea
of a new community born through us, not government, it could only repress
the vagueness through romantic fantasies of a pre-industrial direct democracy.
Tawney's ethical socialism does not solve everything. But it does offer a kind of
concretion to the longing for fraternity, a critique of the present that is at the
same time a guide for individual action. In Tawney's ideal, all work would be a
kind of social service, and each worker would consider himself a professional.

This is, in the first instance, a demand for institution building: in journalism, banking and industry, for instance, vocational schools should instill,
and professional bodies should enforce, a sense of pride in public service and
shame in self-seeking, so that, as Tawney rather quaintly put it, they "cultivate
the *esprit de corps* which is natural to young men, and ... make them feel that to
snatch special advantages for oneself, like any common business man, is, apart
from other considerations, an odious offence against good manners." But it
would also require us to reform existing institutions. For professions can easily
turn guild-like, protecting their members' interests at the expense of society.
The American Medical Association, for example, spent much of the twentieth
century campaigning against proposals to make healthcare cheaper and more ex-
tensive. And there is no doubt that labor unions have sometimes obstructed the
common good. No socialist would ever deny that unions play an essential role
in industrial democracy. But rather than simply defending them uncritically, a
true socialist would hold them to their higher purpose—which is, among other
things, to hold workers to theirs.

But institutions are not everything. Many of us work in trades too diffuse
and diverse for any formal association to serve. And a professional association
is unlikely to have any effect, by itself, unless its members more or less subscribe
to the ethos of service already. There can be professions without professionals,
but there can also be professionals without professions. The final responsibility,
then, lies with individuals. *Change will not come if we wait for some other person or
some other time.*

As we move from an industrial to a service economy, it is becoming easier
to ask yourself what the purpose of your work actually is, what service it actually
performs. Does building your iPhone app count as a genuine service, a contribution to the collective enterprise of society as you see it? Or are you just exploiting
people's weakness for procrastinating? If this seems like a false dichotomy, or if

the notion of work as service seems jejune and naïve, it is because we remain in the grip of Adam Smith's invisible hand. But that grip can be broken—or so I hope to show.

The second part of this essay will be published in Issue Seven.

Jeff Wall, *The Destroyed Room*, 1978
Transparency in lightbox, 159 x 234 cm

MY JOB SEARCH

A MILLENNIAL LOOKS FOR WORK

by Emilie Shumway

O F THOSE HOLDING bachelor's degrees in 2011, 53.6 percent below the age of 25 were either jobless or underemployed. For all but two weeks of the year, I contributed to that statistic. A graduate on an unsuccessful employment tour, I moved from Chicago to D.C. to Colorado to Michigan and finally back to Chicago. Sometimes I was unemployed; sometimes I was underemployed; sometimes I had unpaid internships. I had a total of thirteen interviews across the country, including four over the phone. I purchased four career books. I edited my resume weekly and wrote more than a hundred cover letters.

I flew to New York twice for interviews, once in August of 2010 and then again that December. In the dim evening lighting of the aircraft I studied pages of hypothetical questions and their answers, trying to conjure a person who didn't feel like me. When I touched down, the fast-paced indifference of the city seemed a reflection of the world at the time—uninterested and unwilling to make room. If the city, or the employer, didn't care to admit me, I wanted to force it to.

You can't charm with force, though. When a children's fiction editor asked whether I had a special interest in children's literature, a softball question, I opted for honesty and said I was interested in *all* types of editing. She didn't flinch, exactly, but she filed it away somewhere bad. I wasn't sure what adult really preferred to read and edit *Stellaluna* over a Stephen King thriller, but someone was willing to claim as much, and that person got the job.

Both of my New York interviews were for editorial assistant positions at prominent Times Square-adjacent publishing companies. A New York-based friend counseled against using my Chicago address on resumes, so I used hers instead. I worried my dislocation might seem obvious, that I might break down in questioning, but the topic never came up. The first interview was congenial and unpromisingly easy. The second was carried out by an editor who was visibly bored and clearly had not seen my resume. Both were over in less than thirty minutes.

After moving out to Colorado and settling into a minimum-wage job several months later, I tried my hand at temping, but even there the results were scant. One interviewer said she'd thought I could fill an assistant-type role, but then worried aloud (in a delicate tone) that I lacked the experience. She asked me to take a computer test designed for potential receptionists, which measured my ability to file things alphabetically. The only call I ever received was for a single four-hour stint "inventorying" at Nordstrom Rack.

A month later, I felt particularly optimistic about an interview for a journalism position. When a few days had passed and I'd heard nothing, an ominous wave of defeat washed over me. I would not be getting the job. The next day I called in sick to work, then went to the store and bought an unholy variety of processed desserts. For hours I alternated between eating cookies, sleeping, and watching *The Tudors* on my laptop. By the time my roommate came home I had deteriorated into a sort of hoodied zombie. "I feel like I've been broken up with," I announced. "By my life."

THIS WAS THE horror of graduating circa 2010 with a degree in anything other than computer science. My resume, which seemed to me the objective platform on which I should stand, inexplicably withered from a mountain to a molehill. The reputation of my college, which I chose partially for its prestige, was mysteriously inconsequential. My internships were simply par for the course. My grades were a given. A piece of paper that was meant to convey everything I had to offer professionally was somehow reduced to an accessory. Two feelings overtook me in the wake of this realization: first, powerlessness; then, panic.

Panic maintained a steady presence somewhere in my lower neck region. One day in January, having discovered a second ticket for the expired license on my car (something I couldn't fix immediately, being out of state), I yelled, hit the car, unlocked it, sat down inside, and sobbed hysterically for about half an hour. Unemployed at the time, my money was a tiny, rapidly decreasing pile with failure (if not starvation) waiting at the bottom.

Powerlessness began to erode my self-esteem after only a couple of months. My conception of four years of accomplishments and risks and explorations was floundering even as it was expected to provide the materials from which I would construct and reiterate a professional self. My life's meaning had gone on reserve power, running on memories of pre-graduation, when something like a forward progression still existed. Bursts of anger and self-preservation provided a kind of forward momentum as I hunkered down and churned out applications, but the enthusiasm I was expected to deliver never compared with the immediacy of my barefaced need.

Someone declared insanity to be "doing the same thing over and over and expecting different results"—and this is the job hunt: you apply for jobs again and again, making only slight modifications, and expect different results. You're forced to *have faith* that eventually you'll find someone who will hire you. I often woke up at 2 a.m., heart racing, wondering: "What if I never get a job?" It seemed perilously possible—every application was one of hundreds, and even every interview had a statistically minute chance of working out in my favor. Netting a job requires you to get lucky just once, and what if you never do?

For stretches of time lasting up to a couple months, I went without interviews. It was like deep-sea diving in aimlessness.

I N CONTRAST TO most of us mystified job seekers, the career experts visualize the job hunt as an obstacle course that can be navigated with impersonal precision. When career guidebooks take on interviews, for example, they're reluctant to let you do much thinking on your own. Many exist as a sort of cheat sheet: *101 Great Answers to the Toughest Interview Questions, 301 Smart Answers to Tough Interview Questions, 201 Knockout Answers to Tough Interview Questions* (it never comes down to an even hundred). Some guides recommend simple, physical strategies like a firm handshake or unwavering eye contact. In *The Q&A Manifesto: How to Answer the 45 Most Typical Interview Questions* (the Kindle Edition), self-styled career advisor Landon Long dispenses with any kind of subtlety: "EMPLOYERS WANT TO KNOW YOU ARE GOING TO GENERATE PROFITS!!!" (He goes on to say that you should appear so profitable that hiring anyone else would be "RETARDED.")

In college, I would have rolled my eyes at such half-baked advice; less than a year out, I could be found regularly perusing my bookstore's career section for words of wisdom. Following a string of failures, I began to approach my cover letters with a confusing blend of dread and self-loathing. It was at this time that Martin Yate's *Knock 'em Dead Cover Letters* looked like The Bible, its opening page a gushing sample of testimonials promising nothing short of complete career transformation. A Londoner writes, "I just want to thank you so much for your book. I can really, honestly say that it has influenced my life course!" A Philadelphian proclaims the book "a godsend [that] helped me obtain the job of my dreams eight years ago." A dispassionate Texan just sticks to results: "I was out of work for four months—within five weeks of reading your book, I had four job offers."

Adults do not typically need instruction on how to write letters. But then, in almost every other case, writing letters is an elective experience that is pleasant or (at worst) drearily obligatory (if letters are written at all). Cover letters, meanwhile, require you to be simultaneously tedious and self-aggrandizing. There really isn't much wiggle room here. These are in fact the two elements almost everyone can agree on. You must describe in colorless, adjective-lite detail the work you have done, and you must purport to be impressive for having done it.

For adults with prior work experience, this may not be that difficult: years of legitimate *work* lie in their wake, satisfying moments ready to be cherry-picked and sewn into the easy fabric of a letter. For the recent graduate, however, work experience is either uselessly cerebral or embarrassingly monotonous. The most valuable labor of the college years is typified by midnight breakthroughs on philosophy papers or experiments in the lab, moments in which lengthy, plodding engagement pays off with a sudden handsome display of mental fireworks. To include this moment in a cover letter would be self-indulgent at best, repellent at worst—the personal self is front and center during such an experience, and work takes the form of a mountaintop being slowly scaled. Intellectual growth is a private achievement for a party of one.

Such job applicants are therefore limited to whatever displays of mental acuity can be gleaned from serving coffee or shelving books. The lucky will also have internship experiences similar to mine. I was (in this sense) among the luckiest of recent graduates—I had two pre-graduation internships that were directly related to my careers of interest. Even with this fortunate set up, I approached the blank Word document with trepidation. The language of cover letters retained a "professional" mystique I was hard-pressed to imitate.

Thankfully, the guides usually offer an index page somewhere in their binding with a list of "key verbs," meant to help newbies like me transform something ordinary into something impressive. You didn't move things, you *allocated*. You didn't distribute psychology surveys, you *administered*. By the time I was done, my resume presented me as part machine (generated, compiled), part explorer (navigated, conducted). But my cover letter bragging, mostly a mix of straightforward language arts skills (wrote, edited) and administrative tasks (assisted), gained little from the list.

THE CAREER BOOKS like to pretend that the job hunt is a rational game, one that responds predictably to certain stimuli. This is like saying that if you have clean teeth, smell good, and say nice things on a date, your date will like you. But you typically go into both situations without knowing your counterparts' past experiences, pet peeves, sympathies and physical preferences. *Knock 'em Dead Cover Letters* won't help a whit if someone doesn't feel good about the way you half-smile or sweat through your button-up. My mother, in her pre-interview phone prep, regularly stressed the importance of lipstick. "Wear your hair down," she instructed. "Try to look cute." I once developed a cold sore before an interview, and knew even before walking through the door that my chances were blown.

One of the things career guides love to emphasize is the importance of "putting yourself out there." *Knock 'em Dead* uses the cautionary example of a woman who only passively applies for jobs, insisting that you must follow-up on application materials by "making telephone calls to initiate conversations that must take place to get you job offers." Admittedly, this is sound advice of the dully empowering sort that can easily inspire me. Unfortunately, most companies do little to incentivize *Knock 'em Dead*'s advice. The times I did call, I was met with the gatekeepers of various human resource departments, who seemed cross at my calling and endeavored to get me off the phone as quickly as possible.

Imagining the scenario from their perspective isn't difficult—in this economy, there are literally hundreds of applications per available position; if they set a precedent for rewarding the persistent, they'll spend hours dealing with a barrage of the enthusiastic unemployed for every job that becomes available. The gatekeeping process often goes so far as to enshroud the actual hiring manager in mystery—I liked to imagine him up in the tallest tower of a castle, feverishly tending to a pile of work while an angry, troll-like figure guarded the door. The career books counsel you to always "address your target by name" on cover letters, but very few job postings even make this information available. When I called one company to inquire, I was told simply to use the words "Hiring Manager" in place of a name.

Again, this policy is easy to understand. If the unemployed get a hold of the hiring manager's name, they could conceivably find contact information and, taking the persistence message too much to heart, spam his inbox or call his direct line. Still, the sharp dividing line sets up a situation in which the unemployed person is not only unimportant but actively repugnant in her desperation; on the other end, the employer is not only important but inaccessible and godlike. Unlike the dynamic between expert and (potential) novice, in which the job seeker's inexperience is noted but her person is respected, the servile job seeker now lacks the possibility of unprompted communication with her potential employer, is sometimes blocked from finding his name, can't expect to occupy the manager's mind even when she is scheduled to do so, and is unlikely to receive a notice of rejection.

While inequality is built into the position of one who willingly serves (I never felt slighted, for example, as a barista), the job seeker is mired in a system that is inescapable, and it is only by a feat of unusual empathy that she is extended an olive branch of respect. I recall being shocked after one interview for an ideal position as a music reporter—back in Colorado, again—when the interviewer not only called (called!) to let me down, but offered to recommend me as a freelancer for someone else. Even as he was rejecting me, his humanity in taking the time to reach out provided a much-needed and invigorating jolt to my self-esteem.

Energizing though it was, the experience was one of the few blips in an otherwise unresponsive year. When I came on as an intern at a think tank in D.C., many of the other interns were students at universities in the area. But several of us were schmucky degree-holders, feeling comparatively old, immobilized and desperate. Without exception, we came from other cities. Living off a generous but weary parent donation or off our own savings, we worked for free to buy time while we continued to look for paid jobs. The training was minimal and our positions were designed to support research assistants, who were our age. Over the course of three months, I spoke to my supervisor exactly twice. During my exit interview I spoke to the HR person, whom I'd sat next to at lunch many times, about my interest in a position. The research assistant reassured me I'd have a good shot. My supervisor promised to speak on my behalf.

A few months and several applications later, I was supporting myself on just above minimum wage at a bookstore. The think tank had gone into radio silence. Meanwhile, with each application that I sent out, I began to feel a little more annoying.

M Y STATUS-CONSCIOUS ANXIETY wasn't just an extension of my self-conscious hardwiring or even HR reinforcement; twenty-somethings are the generation that currently dominates the public eye, and quite literally everyone has an opinion on young, unemployed post-grads. In August 2010, the *New York Times Magazine* published the lengthy feature "What Is It About 20-Somethings?" In February 2011, the *Wall Street Journal*'s Kay S. Hymowitz declared twenty-something men to be stuck in a hybrid child-adult purgatory she termed "pre-adulthood" in "Where Have the Good Men Gone?" Around the same time, *Fast Company* took a different approach with "Why Bashing Millennials is Wrong," which cleared the air just in case Millennials didn't know they were near-universally despised. Even this "defense" was a bit of a double-edged sword. The article's author accepts all of the accusations against Millennials—laziness, fickleness, the sense of entitlement—she just believes these traits can be positively exploited. One year later, *New York Magazine* continued the conversation with "The Kids Are Actually Sort of Alright," in which a twenty-something grants that Millennials are "entitled" and "self-absorbed" but points out that at least we're doing as well as we can under the circumstances. It isn't a spectacularly rousing argument.

The consensus seems to be that we Millennials just disappoint, humanity-wise—whether with or without jobs. This is hardly the first time civilization has sounded the alarm on the degradation of the young. Even Aristotle was wringing his hands over the young adults of ancient Greece, whose "hopeful disposition makes them think themselves equal to great things—and that means having exalted notions." I get it. Part of the fun of getting older is earning the right to look down on younger generations.

Still, as an unemployed twenty-something, it has been frustrating to be confronted with this flood of feature articles, many of them written by older folks who lack our experience of having grown up *as* Millennials, in a culture carefully constructed to inspire us. Hazy childhood memories include gazing at "Follow Your Dreams!" posters as a kindergartener, being drafted into Gifted and Talented programs, escaping class to participate in "Young Authors" or "Young Artists" or some similar programmatic nourishment of creativity, and watching television sitcoms and dramas in which the lesson was always some variant of "be yourself." The "self" here was somehow a perfect whole, the dividing lines of "personal" and "professional" unnecessary. To come of age among this cohort, have a dream, and then subdue it, feels cowardly, yet now we are faced with the consensus that we overrate what was fed to us.

In this way, the Millennials are apparently not unlike Aristotle's young Greeks. To grow up beholden to the self, promote your dreams over other life goals, study hard, graduate from college, and then be told you have "an unhealthy sense of entitlement" just for expecting to find an entry-level job is one profoundly mixed cultural message. To expect anything less than "self-absorption" from a person attempting to gain employment and thereby start a life is to expect too much. This is why, with all the complaints about twenty-somethings, the relative silence of the twenty-somethings themselves is worrisome. We've gotten frustrated and pitched tents on Wall Street, but my generation needs more of a voice in the mainstream.

Lately, that voice seems to be coming from Lena Dunham, a 26-year-old Oberlin grad whose 2010 film *Tiny Furniture* spawned an HBO series, which hit the pop culture circuit so hard that it had spawned a wave of overwhelmingly positive reception followed by an immediate backlash even before its second episode. In *Girls* Dunham basically recreates her character from *Tiny Furniture*, fixating on the young, directionless and creatively ambitious female. Her presentation, along with the relationship pitfalls her character stumbles into, rings uncomfortably true. When protagonist Hannah finds herself cut off from her parents and suddenly needing to deal with the very real issue of feeding herself, she gathers her courage and approaches her editor-boss at an unpaid internship of two years. After announcing she can no longer afford "to work for free," the resulting conversation is hilariously and depressingly resonant:

> **BOSS:** Oh, Hannah. I'm sorry to lose you. I was just going to start you manning our Twitter. You have just the quippy voice for that.
> **HANNAH:** Oh, no, no, I'm not quitting. I just um, I know that Joy Lin got hired after interning so I thought that maybe—
> **BOSS:** Hannah. Joy Lin knows Photoshop. Now, in this economy, do you know how many internship requests I get every day?
> **HANNAH:** I would assume a lot.
> **BOSS:** Fifty. It's about fifty. I practically route them into my spam folder. So if you think you have just nothing left to learn from us...
> **HANNAH:** No. It is not that, really, I just, you know, gotta eat.
> **BOSS:** Well, when you get hungry enough, you're gonna figure it out.
> **HANNAH:** Do you mean like physically hungry or like, hungry for the job?
> **BOSS:** I am really gonna miss your energy. I think this is going to be really good for you.

Much has been made of how "privileged" the girls on *Girls* are, but the ease with which Hannah is discarded from a job she's had for two years—immediately following her boss's assertion that she is an "invaluable part of our operation"—is an apt illustration of the gap between the reality of unpaid internships and the cultural notions surrounding their value. As Linda Holmes pointed out on NPR's *Pop Culture Happy Hour*, Hannah is "kind of following the advice that you hear, which is 'Know your own value! Know your own worth! Go out and get it for yourself!'" But when she approaches her boss, his response is essentially "I have an unlimited pool of free labor."

Hannah's "value" is therefore zero. Not because she can't work, but because she's mistakenly bought into a system that countless other young hopefuls have

also bought into: that an unpaid internship will lead to a job. But Hannah's specialization presents perhaps the more pressing problem. Her specific set of skills—writing, editing, identifying artistic merit—are shared by a whole legion of Millennials who "followed [their] dreams" and saw themselves as the Young Artists and Young Authors their third grade teachers took them for. Dream-following therefore led to our whole society of attempted Young Creatives, with supply far exceeding demand. Hannah's skills don't make her one in a million—they make her one *of* a million.

Like Hannah, I bought into this system (despite knowing better). In retrospect, this was embarrassing. But working without payment when I couldn't afford to was embarrassing even at the time, and for simpler reasons; it was an occupation of last resort. Nobody wants to work an unpaid internship out of college.

O F COURSE, REGARDLESS of whether you are getting paid for your work, or doing any work at all for that matter, *Knock 'em Dead* and its ilk will refer to you, the reader, as a professional. The career books make this assumption without knowing you, because, like "special" and "nice," the term has become almost meaningless through dilution. So meaningless that I, an unemployed recent college graduate, was invited to think of myself as a professional.

The dictionary definition of "professionalism" loops back to "profession." Merriam-Webster's fourth noun option, first subcategory, describes a profession as "a calling requiring specialized knowledge and often long and intensive academic preparation." The second subcategory definition is less restrictive: "a principal calling, vocation, or employment." These definitions are revealing in two ways. First, to be considered "professional," one is supposed to be uniquely knowledgeable and intensively prepared—descriptors that apply to very few of the young "professionals" looking for work right out of college.

More tellingly, both definitions suggest that one is primarily "called" to a profession, a description more common to medieval religious awakening than, for example, managing an office. While few would honestly describe their job as a "calling," Merriam-Webster still slips the word in first, reflecting a cultural insistence that transcends the bookstore's career section. (A lazy Amazon.com search for "career" returns results like *Do What You Are: Discover the Perfect Career for You Through the Secrets of Personality Type* and *Career Match: Connecting Who You Are with What You Love to Do.*)

To refer to someone as a "professional" is thus to say the person exists well within her position and also, preferably, that she is mystically matched with it. The problem with this depiction of professionalism is how deeply personal the experiences of feeling "called" to a role and being effortlessly comfortable really are. Both are born of an internal satisfaction so close to the heart as to resemble falling in love—they entail a recognition, an ease of looking at something and seeing yourself reflected back.

Yet the job hunt, as I gradually realized, requires you to construct a "professional" identity that emphasizes certain qualities—confidence, enthusiasm, assertiveness—at complete odds with what you, as a bewildered, unemployed twenty-something, are likely to be feeling. The interview, in particular, is largely a test to see whether you can divide your personal self from this newly minted "professional" self. Often it begins with an ambiguous invitation to "tell me about yourself," which is newspeak for "don't tell me anything personal about yourself." Once, before I came to understand the expectation behind this question (*reiterate your resume*), I began with a lengthy preamble about going to a mediocre high school, reading a lot, knowing there was more out there, getting into a celebrated private college, etc. I was telling the interviewer a tale of my *personal* self, a truncated but cherished narrative of my ambitious nature and very tame rise to glory. It didn't even occur to me at the time to trot out my professional self, because I didn't have a professional self to trot out.

Meanwhile, culturally, the personal and professional selves are continuously conflated. Televised representations of professionals span wildly across the board; *Parks and Recreation*'s Leslie Knope is a mid-level government employee so assuredly "called" to her position that her love of meetings and paperwork is a constant gag on the show. She represents a professional who sees no division between her personal and professional selves, as the personal favorites on the walls of her office—Madeleine Albright and Hillary Clinton—are also her professional heroes. Even through a political campaign, the more personal aspects of her identity end up making her a stronger professional.

On the other side of the spectrum, *Mad Men*'s Don Draper is a professional whose personal life remains, for the most part, a tightly guarded secret from his colleagues. His knack for advertising makes it appear to be a kind of "calling," but his deeper, darker secrets mean he's never quite comfortable (though he usually appears to be). What distinguishes Don as a professional is, in large part, his privacy—his personality weakens him professionally, while Leslie's strengthens her.

Draper and Knope are diametrically opposed in their decisions to involve themselves personally with their careers, yet both are protagonists on shows that privilege the relationship between career and personal life perhaps above any other. To watch either show is to leave the television with an awareness that a career is a major part of life—perhaps the truest love story—but with entirely different ideas of what it means to actually be a professional.

ATTEMPTING TO FIRST understand, and then cleave, one's professional and personal selves is complicated by the ways in which the professional self crowds in on the personal self, first dictating one's feelings and then emanating outward. Among the four "supportive communication skills" listed by *Knock 'em Dead* are "grooming and dress," "social graces," and "body language." The online resources provided by the guide include a link to an About.com listing of grooming tips for women. The recommendations suggest that dressing for the office can be a minefield of *faux pas*. Women should not wear jewelry which is "too large," earrings should always be "above the earlobe," perfume is to be avoided, businesswomen should wear a "nice, conservative wrist watch," and, perhaps most alarmingly, "wearing no makeup at all is almost as bad as wearing too much makeup."

One identity crisis I didn't see coming presented itself the January afternoon I stood paralyzed in a Macy's, staring down a rack of blazers and weighing my options. I'd just gotten the think tank internship in D.C., and the dilemma concerned whether or not I needed to buy a blazer for the position. The weight of the question wasn't in the uncertainty, but rather down the rabbit hole of implications and assumptions I'd need to make about myself if I indeed needed to buy the blazer. *I am not the sort of person who wears a blazer*, I agonized. Even the salesgirl seemed to sense my apparently pointless misery as she handed me new options: "Are these not working for you?"

It wasn't that I looked down on blazer-clad professionals, but rather that the blazer suddenly symbolized everything about an entire adult world that I didn't identify with and, since I was worming my way into it, felt troublingly alienated from. At no point up until the age of 23 did I envision myself wearing a blazer, and buying one now made me feel like I was walking through the wrong door.

For as long as I can remember, I've wanted to be a writer. This was a satisfying enough ambition in high school, and I filled enough notebooks with stories and terrible poetry to imagine I would make good on it, but the idea began to break apart in college. Living off your creativity began to seem like the delicious destiny of either the overwhelmingly talented or the independently wealthy, and

I was neither. What I knew was that millions of jobs existed that children never dreamed of, but they had to be carried out by sacrificial adults nevertheless. I would start in one of those positions, I told myself, and then transition into my dream. The other thing I knew—whispered by the same nervous voice that kept me from a degree in creative writing—was that there didn't seem to be enough space for everyone to realize their dreams. It is telling that so few Young Creatives make their way into the public's awareness, while those who find success are the ones feeding those very same impulses. Instagram—a type of software that makes even your most ordinary photos look old-timey and nostalgic—was sold to Facebook for a billion dollars. Even Joy Lin knows Photoshop.

Knowing that I was entering the job market as a means of biding my time—that I would "figure things out" once I had a full-time position—didn't make the transition any easier. How long would I defer what I really wanted to do? In truth, some tiny part of me, deep in denial, understood why I had so much trouble getting a job. Since the age of fifteen I'd seen the adult world as being full of people languishing eight hours a day in a state of detached psychical gloom, people tending less and less to their ever-shrinking raisins in the sun. I would have considered cutting off a limb to get hired, and at the same time, the last thing I wanted was to restrict my jewelry, buy a wristwatch, don a blazer, bury my dreams, and start an adult life.

I WENT FROM PRESTIGIOUS internship to temporary bookseller. Antique lamps replaced fluorescent lights, bathing me in a dreamlike glow. I was once again wearing jeans to work, making money in laughably small amounts, and allowed to be mainly a personal self by day. In my off hours, I practiced being a professional through an endless stream of applications and a few interviews.

As the blazer incident taught me, the professional and personal selves are seldom as easily separable as convenience would suggest. The degree of overlap is not insignificant—factors like enthusiasm, choice of earrings, and tone are all deeply rooted in my personal experience and mood, and consequently part of me feels violated in their unnatural appropriation by professionalism. If my professional self was an enacted rewiring of my personal self, how could my personal self remain unaffected? The need to emote enthusiasm professionally had the odd effect of neutering it personally.

Knock 'em Dead and its brethren are not, strictly speaking, wrong. Their advice is often reasonable, helpful, even (in some cases) precisely correct. But in spoon-feeding you selves that aren't *your* self, they erode a sense of identity already pale with rejection. The most useful how-to career guide I could have found wouldn't have been for cover letters or resumes or interviews; it would have been an instruction manual for getting through the job hunt with my confidence intact. It would have pointed out that interviewers often ignore the interviewee not because of any strong negative opinion, but rather because people are sometimes careless and rude. It would have parted the curtain on the litany of tiny mistakes and offenses the employed person unintentionally commits, to little consequence, throughout her career. It would have drawn upon the largely sympathetic collective outlook of the employed on the unemployed in this economy and reminded me that Americans love a comeback. Finally, it would have questioned whether I was really going to let the search for a job scare me into a new sense of self.

Last winter, I finally threw away full-time underemployment and bit the bullet, quitting my job at the bookstore and moving in with my parents, with the intention of devoting myself full-time to the job search. As I sat at home and churned through dozens of applications a day, I began to experience a dissociation; the more applications I methodically sent out, the less time I spent second-guessing my presentation. Applying to fifteen jobs a day, and contacting five people in an attempt to network, less of me went into the process. I could have examined whether these cover letters were really perfect, or fretted over the likelihood of getting responses from those I emailed, or, quite simply, I could have *not*.

In the comfort of my childhood home, drinking my parents' coffee and watching movies with them as they serenely accepted me back into their lives, I could finally see my unemployment as they saw it—a phase in passing, and nothing to panic over. If someone in New York balked at my professional representation, life went on. Dinner still needed to be made, the dishes still needed to be washed. I woke up and went to bed with my personal self, who began to care less and less about the tension with its professional counterpart.

What saved me in the last month of searching for jobs was allowing myself this personal detachment from my professional self. The two didn't have to entirely mesh or separate; they just had to exist, side by side, in some (necessarily imperfect) form. My work experience no longer became a representation of me, my inability to get a job no longer a reflection of my worth. They were both just facts, disembodied. I did what I've done. I knew what they wanted. I could do the job as well as anyone else. If they weren't interested, they could join the crowd.

After a few weeks, I got an interview. I hopped on a train and rode four hours to the city, slept on my friend's couch, and prepared the next morning by answering prospective interview questions in my notebook. I had lunch with a friend in the same industry, who briefed me on the job description and explained what would matter to the employers. It was the least nervous interview I've ever had. And I got the job.

DICTIONARY OF RECEIVED IDEAS

AMERICAN POLITICS ADDENDUM

by Justin Evans

EDITOR'S NOTE: IT will appear that some definitions are directly contradictory, that, for instance, the national debt cannot be simultaneously the fault of the incumbent and his challenger. However, recent research has discovered—*pace* the old authoritarian certainties of the past—that, like men & women, homosexuals & bisexuals & heterosexuals, blacks & whites, the peoples of the various political parties in fact have different epistemologies, so that, just as all truths are only truths for someone, so political truths are likewise for someone. We must respect and value their diverse perspectives on our beautiful world. So-called "contradictions" (the hobgoblin of small minds) are in fact the result of these differing epistemological standpoints with regard to the "real world" (which is, of course, nothing other than the product of those many standpoints); to pretend otherwise is only to imperiously colonize the hearts and minds of others.

American Dream: that anyone born in the U.S.A. can become rich enough to be President.

Atheists: not a significant interest group

Bipartisanship: i) guarantees a good outcome (2008); ii) unacceptable compromise (2010); iii) guarantees no outcome (2012).

Business: i) good; ii) defined by economists as self-interested rational agent.

Catholics: vote for Mormons

Citizen: defined by economists as self-interested rational agent.

Debt, national: i) my opponent's fault; ii) my predecessor's fault; iii) not connected to economy, international.

Democratic Party, policy of: ERROR—NULL SET

Economist: objective scientist.

Economy, domestic: i) my opponent's fault; ii) nothing to do with the international economy; iii) China's fault; iv) can be helped by reforming school system, immigration law, public infrastructure and health insurance system.

Economy, international: Europeans' fault.

Electability: combination of obscene wealth, average demeanor and below-average morality.

Evangelical Christians: vote for Catholics

Founding Fathers: i) group of men ranging from Sam Smith to John Calhoun; ii) all agree with you.

Government: i) a business; ii) bad.

Mainline Protestants: Europeans

Money: i) time; ii) power; iii) speech.

Mormons: cult

Nation-state: a really, really, really, really, really big household.

Politician: defined by economists as self-interested rational agent.

Republican Party, policy of: libertarianism without liberty.

Reform: oppose at least four of the following reforms—school system; health insurance; public infrastructure; immigration law; repeal of the Burnt Toast & MacGuffin Act of 1823.

Super PAC: organizations that further the principles of democracy, set up in accordance with guidelines laid down by the Founding Fathers.

Two party system: ignore the inconsistency of a two party system operating under a constitution written for a political system with no parties.

Washington: i) hero; ii) city in one of 27 states, 1 district, three foreign countries—in two separate counties, two provinces, and 4 barangays; iii) lake; iv) mountain; v) bridge; vi) park; vii) island; viii) boulevard; ix) avenue; x) street; xi) university in 7 states; xii) high schools everywhere; xiii) 2-4 CTA stations; xiv) Amtrak station in MO; xv) bomber; xvi) ocean liner; xvii) submarine (forthcoming); xviii) Presbytery; xix) Wizards; xx) Capitals; xxi) Redskins (sic); xxii) Nationals; xxiii) Huskies; xxiv) monument syndrome; xxv) state; xxvi) incompetent, enigmatic, taciturn general; xxvii) symbol of American politics.

symposium
what are animals for?

Katie Kline, *East Village*, 2010

CAVE TROUT

by Fabien Tepper

During a stop on a cross-country drive this year, I watched a crowd of long, pale fish erupt from the surface of the Lost Sea, the hemisphere's largest underground lake. They were rainbowless rainbow trout, and a young boatman was lobbing fistfuls of food at them, deep below a hill at the edge of Sweetwater, Tennessee. They were not, he explained, native to the lake. As he spoke, a trout sailed past the ear of a teenager next to me, provoking screams and a lurch in our glass-bottomed tourist raft. Predecessors of these fish had been carried down through Craighead Caverns and released into the lake by people curious to see if they would escape and reveal a conduit to another body of water. But they stayed put. And in the deep, lightless cave their eyesight and color faded and their sex drive vanished. Since the lake itself sustains no plant or animal life, the trout learned to swarm around visiting rafts and launch themselves into airborne food deliveries. "Now we restock them and keep them on as a tourist attraction," concluded the boatman. A memorable end-of-tour splash.

It was unsettling to imagine their lives. Where rainbow trout occur naturally, they have a lot to do: they control dragonfly populations, forage, mate, host colonies of parasitic slime mold, feed bears and provide memorable stories to fishermen. They are bursting with nutritional and ecological value to others. But the trout of the Lost Sea were separated from every external life form, every meteorological pattern and almost every activity around which their species has evolved. They didn't spawn, and after hours they had nothing to hunt, gather or see. A writer for *Chattanooga Parent* described them as "ghostly monsters." Were they good for nothing more than spooking tourists into a gift-shoppy delirium? Seeing those wan cave dwellers sealed off from so much of their value to others, I wondered what made their lives worthwhile to them. Could any of a trout's satisfactions remain unassailed by the indignities of a bugless, bearless, lightless, idle life?

Some of us feel that our own lives are inherently valuable, regardless of how much anyone else may cherish, need, hate or snub us. Whether we are social reformers, corporate peons or volatile drunks, most of us find the quality and continuation of our lives to be very important. But it's hard to pinpoint what makes up one's "inherent value," and people sometimes use the term more emphatically than precisely. Awed people, for example, sometimes speak of inherent or intrinsic value. Of a sculpture so heartbreaking that pricing it seems crass. Of a feline whose grace and ecological importance are too complex to fully understand, let alone quantify. But in those cases, I think, the awestruck are mistaking intangible value, which resists being precisely quantified, for inherent value. The beauty of a sculpture may be priceless, but it can be squarely located in the eyes of beholders. And an ocelot's role as a keystone predator is a function that *others* depend on; when she is locked behind zoo bars, she is no longer valuable in the same way.

Inherent value is something that emerges not from outside admiration, but from the capacity for well-being. A wondrous painting may not have any such value, yet many of the world's less distinguished dwellers—dull people, ubiquitous pigeons—somehow do, whether or not anyone admires them. Dutch ethicists Bart Rutgers and Robert Heeger call an animal's inherent value its "own good," and locate it within the life she can live. "Animals have ends and purposes that are characteristic to them," they write. "They are oriented by themselves towards the development of species-characteristic abilities and the fulfillment of their needs." Here they echo an Aristotelian concept introduced into animal policy discussions by American veterinary ethicist Bernard Rollin, who in 1993 predicted a change in the U.S. social consensus on animal welfare: "Not only will welfare mean control of pain and suffering," he wrote, "it will also entail nurturing and fulfillment of the animals' natures"—their *telos*. True to Rollin's forecast, over the past twelve years the Humane Society of the United States has thwarted powerful agricultural lobbies to reform calf, chicken and sow husbandry in eight states by convincing voters and legislators with this argument: "Animals built to move should be allowed to move."

As I write this I am sitting in a sun-soaked adobe courtyard in Albuquerque, beside sky-straining tulips and cacti. A small terrier trots by, nostrils aloft, while I try to press my thoughts into a tidy shape. A breeze ruffles my hair and his. It occurs to me that life forms are constantly engaged in processes of change (consuming, converting, growing, learning, bonding), so that we never cease to be full of unrealized potentials. With this in mind, Rutgers and Heeger point out that animals' "prospects and development" stand to be harmed or benefitted, alongside their health and comfort. Our understanding of inherent value should, then, include these prospects—a sleeping otter's potential for play, a beaten dog's potential to learn trust, a zoo-bound elephant's potential to walk for miles. Change, as many have pointed out, is life's only constant. We animals

long for some changes, while others—like puberty—descend upon us, upending our tastes, impulses and bodies. So our understanding of what makes others' lives worthwhile would be crippled if we ignored the potentials and needs that dwell in their changes.

I propose that someone's inherent value is her own potential to exercise, thrive and bask in her natural sensations and abilities. The capacity to flex her mind and body, organize, learn from injury, luxuriate in sunlight or water, stretch her fibers, scratch itches or build a home. Inherent value inhabits the leg-wending of a cat, the herding fervor of a border collie, the sunning of a snake. A cow, penguin or woman sheltering her fuzz-topped infant. A horse scratching her belly over a bush, a wolf joining his pack in a howl, a monkey timing her leap onto a swinging branch, a bowerbird weaving found snippets of blue into his courtship tent.

KOI VS. TUNA

A week after sailing the Lost Sea I visited a friend's family at a home that included an outdoor pond of koi fish, some as large as ground hogs. Here was another motley crew of transplants living in an isolated pool and depending on humans for food. Yet it wasn't nearly as hard to imagine what made their lives satisfying. I watched the fish swim toward me with tendrilled mouths gaping, swerve at the pond's edge, scoop up a few crepey elm seeds that had rained into their pool, and spit them out again. These fish could see, mate, roll things around in their mouths and sense the passage of days, seasons, animals. I felt their gazes flicker across me as I enjoyed their bright colors, broad shoulders and round bellies, the smooth arterial walls of their open mouths.

When I asked my friend's mother, keeper of the koi, what they were for, she did not miss a beat. "They encourage meditative mindfulness," she replied. "If I spent more time watching the fish, I would have a spiritual life." She said the koi were "messengers from another world" whose surfacings offered a window into an ineffable other kind of being. Within that mystique lay both a lesson for humans— "You are one of many. There is no pride of place."—and the promise of a deeper wisdom: "Fish *know*."

"And then there are the fish you eat," she added, "which are not messengers from the other world; they are tuna sandwiches in the making."

Those koi and tuna have their work cut out for them. Together, their anointed roles— messenger, sage, sandwich filling—are an illustrative cross section of the uses humans find for other animals. While our inherent value hinges on our potential to thrive, our vast instrumental value depends on our potential to serve others. We animals use each other in concrete, commodifiable ways: for transportation, food, exercise, company and protection; as hosts and as slaves. The enterprising homo sapiens has expanded that list through leather whips, internet hunting, zoo exhibits and squads of bomb-sniffing dogs. We also mine the animal world for intangible values; French anthropologist Claude Levi-Strauss pointed to its intellectual value when he wrote that "animals are good to think with." We use our non-human cousins as totems, icons, villains and mascots; as signifiers of wealth and prowess, tradition and communion—infinite fodder

for the construction of our own identities. In a recent issue of *Mother Earth News*, American woodsman David Petersen invoked several of these values to explain why he hunted: "I am proud of procuring that wild meat myself, no middlemen needed or wanted, thank you— keeping alive ancient skills that were part of the evolution of our unique species through thousands of generations, relying on personal effort and knowledge (the good old-fashioned term here is 'woodsmanship') and our evolved, predatory instincts rather than on the store-bought, space-age technology so popular with misguided hunters today." When Petersen hunts, it's not just meat he's after.

CREEPING THINGS AND CROSSING GUARDS

The world's religions and philosophers vary widely in how they attribute inherent and instrumental value. The God of the Judeo-Christian Old Testament endows humans with inherent value by creating them in his image, and then grants them dominion "over every creeping thing that creepeth upon the earth," enshrining the assumption that the main value of non-humans is instrumental. The God of the Muslim Qur'an, on the other hand, acknowledges the parallel lives of humans and non-humans—"There is not an animal on the earth, nor a being that flies on its wings, that does not form communities like you"—and even warns against harming beasts of burden, like the camel: "Let her graze freely in God's earth. Do not touch her with bad intentions, or you will get caught in painful retribution." And in the Buddhist sutras, little distinction is made between the earth's species—all are capable of achieving enlightenment; all are interchangeable through reincarnation.

Over the past half-millennium, as evolving theories of human and animal rights have been codified in various constitutions, the focus of philosophers has generally moved toward the inherent value end of the spectrum. In the seventeenth century, French philosopher René Descartes exerted a lasting influence on Europeans' views of non-human animals by calling them "automata" and explaining their cries during vivisection as nothing more than the grinding of misaligned cogs. To Descartes, a dog could neither speak nor think nor feel and therefore had nothing—neither a soul nor inherent value—to complicate the head-on pursuit of her instrumental value to scientists. German philosopher Immanuel Kant, though he stressed the need to defend human dignity at all costs, saw no dignity in non-humans. He did believe that we have a duty to treat animals mercifully, but only because we have an obligation to develop our capacity for mercy; we must practice for when it matters.

As I continue writing at another outdoor café, a printed coffee receipt has caused my own mercy to flex unexpectedly. Curled into a perfect tube, the slip has puffed off my table, rolled diagonally across the sidewalk, and hopped into a parking lot. Lifted by rising gusts of wind, it rolls between the wheels of several cars and emerges at the far end of the lot, where it somersaults into a hard patch of sand, pivots and launches in another direction. Enchanted by its long trip, I find myself worrying that a pair of feet might round the nearest street corner and crush the little loop. As I ponder this strange anxiety, I can trace it to a memory: last year I spent several rapt and protective minutes watching as a praying mantis crossed a steep human foot path at a Buddhist monastery I was visiting. The thick-armed insect stopped and whipped its head around twice when others took flash photos, turned back to its path, and proceeded its slow labor across the asphalt until a speed-walker pushed through the gathered observers and crushed it underfoot. I gasped; the walker vanished uphill, unaware; the mantis thrashed to unbend its broken skeleton.

To my eye the mantis had appeared cautious, deliberate, and then terrified—well-deserving of moral consideration, and of a better crossing guard than I. The dance of the little receipt, on the other hand, seems to have tricked me. Its sparrow-like movements have tripped my habitual concern for little animals underfoot, even though I know that the loop has nothing to lose and no inherent value. I may be the only creature alive who would lament its flattening. But for reasons that Kant might appreciate, I don't think my worry was wasted. A nun once suggested to me that treading delicately on the ground—lowering each foot with utmost gentleness—was a useful focus for a walking meditation. It was sound advice: not because the ground itself is sensitive to the force of my steps, but because it allows me to practice minding the impact of my most casual actions. Unlike Descartes, I assume that many non-human animals can think, feel and hurt. But like Kant, I assume that caring for non-humans—a dog, a loop, a velveteen rabbit—develops vital faculties like empathy and responsibility. Perhaps all of us animals, and even the earth beneath us, share this instrumental value: we provide practice targets for empathetic animals.

In eras following Kant's, Australian ethicist Peter Singer and Englishman Jeremy Bentham—whose inanimate but cherished walking cane named "Dapple," incidentally, rests forever tucked between the knees of his seated, dressed skeleton on display in London—argued for the merciful treatment of non-human animals for their own sake. Both philosophers are consequentialists, meaning they evaluate moral decisions by weighing the good and bad outcomes of any choice. "The question is not 'can they reason?' nor 'can they speak?' but 'can they suffer?'" wrote Bentham in 1789, critiquing Descartes' and Kant's bases for the moral exclusion of animals. Two hundred years later Singer galvanized the modern animal rights movement with his book *Animal Liberation* (1975), which looked at the emerging practices of industrialized animal farming in light of the harm and benefit they caused; he found that human consumption of most animal products—oysters apart—caused vastly more harm than good. Perhaps another way to see consequentialist arguments is that they weigh our instrumental and inherent values against one another.

American philosopher Tom Regan shows an even deeper concern with inherent value, in opposing the exploitation of animals because of their rights, not just their pain. We and many other animals have inherent value because what happens to us matters to us, he argues; we are "subjects of a life." "We want and prefer things, believe and feel things, recall and expect things." And however much instrumental value we may hold for others, all of us subjects of a life have the right not to be treated merely as the means to another's end.

And yet we treat other humans as means to our own ends all the time, without offending common sensibilities about fairness—when we hitch a ride, sell something or dress to turn heads. Perhaps there should be a distinction between use and exploitation. If I seek out someone's good company, I am gently using him to further my own well-being, and hopefully his as well. But if I instead hurt him in the process—if I make him listen to painful anecdotes, or detain him from an important date, or eat him—that's exploitation. By this standard, many of the ways we use other animals—in circuses, research labs, zoos and farms—become harder to defend.

DISEMBATTLING

Moral battles over how humans should treat other animals are usually waged between those who defend our right to use natural resources and those who defend animals' right to live free of exploitation; the two sides, unsurprisingly, argue on different terms. They remain entrenched because lives and traditions are at stake, and because each is rooted in a fundamental truth.

Those defending our use of non-human animals are right that human evolution, history and identity have been deeply bound up in that use—especially in our use of animals who could be made to work for us. The empires of China, Persia, Egypt and Rome grew into sophisticated hegemonies through the trade borne by horses and camels across the Silk Route. Anthropologists have credited the viability of early animal agriculture to domestic dogs, and the colonial dominance of Eurasians to their continent's vast share of the world's large domesticable mammals. On the other hand, those defending the rights of non-human animals are correct that over the same arc of centuries, humans have eloquently justified using other humans for a similar range of empire-building purposes—as slaves, trophies, weapons and mascots. And collectively, we often find these sacrifices to be not only unjustified by their place in history, but the subjects of its most shameful chapters.

While traveling across the U.S., I have collected some off-the-cuff responses to the question, "what are animals for?" Some people were irritated by the implication that animals are for anything. "What are they *for*? They're for themselves. What do you even mean? We're animals—what are we 'for?'" demanded an Irish ESL teacher around a hostel dinner table. Others accepted the premise and offered thoughtful lists. A friend from Mexico who conducts diabetes research on cloned mice, suggested that "food, company and healing are probably the three main things they're for, right?" A small-scale chicken farmer in Ohio saw our purpose as clearly dictated by our evolutionary drives: above all, survive and reproduce. "What is a squirrel's real purpose?" he asked, in an online conversation. "To reduce the number of tree saplings. To feed predators. They're cogs in an ecosystem. So are we. That's an existential purpose—filling a niche. Doing our jobs."

That farmer got me thinking: some of us, like the Lost Sea trout, are fairly detached from ecosystems, and many of us owe traits to artificial selection. Smash-faced pugs. A factory pig too fat for sex. All of us with arranged marriages or slavery in our bloodlines. When someone interferes with our survival or reproduction, does adapting to our captors' needs then become our purpose in life? "Unfortunately, yes," replied the farmer, and as an example he gave the grassy ancestor of maize. "By altering it ... we have changed its ecological role whether the maize likes it or not." Someone who has experienced captivity might object to his extrapolation from maize to humans, but he is right that

artificial selection changes instrumental values; that's why we do it.

And how about the other part of purpose—does inherent value also change under the genetic knife? Another Dutch ethicist, Frans Brom, writes, "We are able to change the functioning of an animal, in such a way that we may take away the capacity to have certain experiences. The idea that we deprive animals from certain possible good experiences, without causing suffering, does not seem to fit in with the idea of 'intrinsic value.'" This raises an interesting question about how to respect inherent value: Is it enough to ensure that we animals are fully able to exercise our bodies and minds? Or should we also protect each other from genetic meddlings into the very nature of the exercise we crave?

If so, where is the moral line between humans' studied tampering with animals, and all of the other ways species change each other? Perhaps it should distinguish exchanges built around confinement from those which leave survivors free to learn and adapt. Deer have learned to bound away from stalking hunters but eat from the hands of gawking tourists. Hermit crabs whose shells have received an electric shock sit tight until a new shell rolls around—and then rush to switch homes. And dogs' winning sensitivity to humans appears linked to the first blooms of mutualism that sprang up when our two species met at the edges of early human encampments, trading food scraps for sentry work. As we negotiated our terms, each species may have favored members of the other group who were friendly and trusting, with good instincts for cross-species communication. Now that those relationships have ripened for a few thousand generations, humans have evolved an uncanny skill at interpreting the emotional timbres of recorded, unfamiliar barks. And dogs—but not wolves—have learned to read our intentions through our tiniest eye movements. It is no coincidence that so many dogs revel in human companionship, while their wild cousins remain aloof. Dogs' *teloi*, the basis of their inherent value, have changed through these relationships, as have ours.

Katie Kline, *Palm Desert*, 2009

ON KILLING ANIMALS

by Gary Francione

Every year, the Virginia Department of Agriculture and Consumer Services releases data on the number of animals killed at the Commonwealth's animal shelters, including the facility operated by People for the Ethical Treatment of Animals (PETA), located in Norfolk, Virginia. And every year, PETA kills a higher percentage of animals than are killed at most of the "kill" shelters located throughout the country.

The 2011 numbers were certainly disturbing. PETA reported that out of the 2,050 animals that it took in (1,214 cats; 778 dogs; 58 "other" companion animals), it killed 1,965 (1,198 cats; 713 dogs; 54 "others"). That's an overall kill rate of almost 96 percent, with 91 percent for dogs and almost 99 percent for cats. According to the American Society for the Prevention of Cruelty to Animals, the national kill rate at shelters is 60 percent for dogs and 70 percent for cats.

PETA's kill rate would be high if it were a traditional "kill" shelter. But it promotes itself as an animal rights group; indeed, it claims to be "the largest animal rights organization in the world, with more than 3 million members and supporters" and states that it "has always been known for uncompromising, unwavering views on animal rights."

How can an animal rights group kill *any* animals, much less kill *more* animals than plain-vanilla shelters that have no pretense to being animal rights organizations?

PETA suggests that it only kills animals when they are suffering and there is no alternative. But elsewhere it has acknowledged that it has been killing healthy and adoptable animals for some years now. For instance, in 1991 it killed a group of rabbits and roosters at a shelter it had at that time, claiming a lack of money to care for the animals. So even if we assume that some of the animals that PETA kills are suffering and cannot be saved, at least some, and probably many, are healthy animals. How can this be?

The usual responses are less than satisfying. The Center for Consumer Freedom (CCF) maintains a website, PETA Kills Animals, which claims that PETA is just engaged in outright deception by maintaining a "slaughterhouse operation" at the same time as it peddles a "phony 'animal rights' message." But then CCF is an organization that lobbies on behalf of the fast-food, meat, alcohol and tobacco industries, so (because PETA has a somewhat antagonistic relationship with the fast-food and meat industries) it would be unrealistic to look to CCF for anything other than inflammatory rhetoric.

Some animal advocates try to attribute PETA's activity to psychopathology, claiming that its co-founder, Ingrid Newkirk, harbors "dark impulses" and is a "'disturbed person,' a 'shameless animal killer,' and the executrix of a 'bloody reign' of terror over dogs and cats"; Newkirk is even compared to "nurses who get a thrill from killing their human patients."* Putting aside the hyperbole here, in a very large organization like PETA it is unlikely that the policy on killing animals can be a manifesta-

---

* See James McWilliams, "PETA's Terrible, Horrible, No Good, Very Bad History of Killing Animals," in the *Atlantic* (March, 2012).

tion of any one person's alleged personality characteristics.

•

I am not reluctant to criticize PETA and have done so extensively in the past. But I believe that there is an issue at stake much more fundamental than PETA's ostensible inconsistency. There is, and forgive the pun, an 800-pound theoretical gorilla in the room whose existence is being ignored by all of us.: Is what PETA is doing in painlessly killing dogs, cats and other animals, at least some of whom are healthy and adoptable, actually inconsistent with the "animal rights" position?

In order to answer that question, it is necessary to identify what the animal rights position is, or, at least, what it is commonly understood to be. And to do that we need to turn to the position of Peter Singer, the Australian philosopher whose 1975 book *Animal Liberation* is rightly or wrongly credited with moving us all from the animal welfare era into the animal rights era. We are told time and time again: "The modern animal rights movement may be dated to the 1975 publication of *Animal Liberation* by Australian philosopher Peter Singer."

It is important to understand two things about Singer from the outset. First, he is a utilitarian. Utilitarianism is the theory that what is morally right or wrong depends on consequences; the right act or policy is that which will result in the best consequences for all affected. In assessing consequences, we must be impartial and give equal consideration to everyone's happiness or pleasure or other interests, without regard to race, sex, sexual orientation, intellectual or physical abilities and so on. Singer's primary contribution is to argue that species should be regarded as morally irrelevant just like race or sex, so that we should not undervalue animal interests based solely on species. But this does not make Singer an *animal rights* theorist. Utilitarians reject the notion of moral rights because, as we will see as this discussion continues, rights protect the right holder even if the balance of consequences does not favor that protection. So although Singer is characterized as "the father of the animal rights movement," Singer does not propose a theory of animal rights at all.

Second, and following from the first point, Singer does not maintain that animals have a moral right to life. But, more importantly, Singer has often expressed the view that many species do not even have an *interest* in their lives, because they exist in a sort of "eternal present." He has recently acknowledged that at least some of those species may in fact have mental continuity but he has thus far failed to recognize that they have the same kind of morally significant interest in continued existence that he accords to humans, nonhuman great apes, marine mammals and elephants, and that would make veganism a moral imperative. Singer continues to maintain that it is morally defensible to eat animals so long as they are provided a reasonably pleasant life and a relatively painless death, and he supports the advocacy efforts of large organizations that promote "happy" animal use. In short, Singer continues to promote the notion that the primary problem with animal exploitation is not *that* we use them but *how* we use them.

PETA claims that all the animals that they kill are killed painlessly. The animals are, in all likelihood, not suffering; they are surely dying a better death than they would if they were "food" animals being slaughtered at any federally inspected slaughterhouse. And, truth be told, PETA is probably delivering a better death to these animals than they would get at most animal shelters.

So if we assume that animals do not have an interest in continuing to live, and if PETA is, as a factual matter, not imposing pain and suffering on animals when they are killed, then what PETA is doing is not in any conflict with Peter Singer's position.

•

According to Singer, then, animals, or at least many of them, do not care that we use and kill them; they just care about how they are treated when we use and kill them. At this point, you are probably asking where Singer could have gotten this idea. But it turns out that his position not only has a long history but—and here comes the big surprise—*is one that is actually shared by most people.*

Put aside dogs and cats for a second. Ask yourself: how do *you* feel about the morality of animal use for the meat, dairy products and eggs you consume?

The chances are that you share the conventional wisdom that has been the cornerstone of western thinking for 200 years now when it comes to animal use: that it is morally acceptable to use and kill animals for human purposes so long as we treat animals "humanely" and do not impose "unnecessary" suffering on them. Suffering matters; killing, as long as it is not accompanied by suffering, does not.

But then our conventional wisdom is really no different from Singer's position, the one that informs PETA's actions. We may get upset about what PETA does but that has more to do with how we fetishize dogs and cats than with the morality of killing animals. Putting aside dogs and cats, most people agree with PETA that an animal death without pain and suffering is morally acceptable. The primary difference between PETA and Singer, on the one hand, and everyone else, on the other, is that the former think that the "humane" treatment standard requires a great deal more than the latter does. But this is basically a quantitative matter, not a qualitative one.

Why are we so comfortable with the idea that animals, as a factual matter, have an interest in not suffering but do not have an interest in continuing to live? What is the source of our conventional wisdom on this matter?

The answer requires that we go back several hundred years. Before the nineteenth century, animals were, for all intents and purposes, excluded from the moral and legal community. As a matter of our social, moral and legal institutions, we did not regard animals as beings to whom we could have direct obligations. Animals were just *things*; neither our use nor our treatment of animals mattered morally or legally. There were some who, like French philosopher René Descartes, claimed that animals were literally nothing more than machines. He called them "automatons." Descartes denied that animals were sentient; that is, he did not believe as a factual matter that animals were perceptually aware and able to have conscious experiences, including the experience of pain. They were just like machines created by humans, except they were created by God.

For the most part, however, it was accepted by almost everyone else, including Aquinas, Aristotle, John Locke and Immanuel Kant, that animals are sentient and have an interest in avoiding pain and suffering. But these thinkers argued that we could ignore animal interests and treat animals *as if* they were Cartesian machines because they were different from humans in that they were supposedly not rational or self-aware, not able to think in terms of abstract concepts or use symbolic communication, incapable of engaging in reciprocal moral relationships with humans or not in possession of a soul.

However, regardless of whether humans regarded nonhumans as machines that were not sentient and had no interests, or as sentient and with interests that could be ignored because of supposed cognitive or spiritual defects, the bottom line remained the same: we could not have direct moral or legal obligations to animals. We could have obligations that concerned animals, such as an obligation not to damage our neighbor's cow, but that obligation was owed to the neighbor as the owner of the cow, not to the cow. The cow simply did not matter morally or legally.

All of this changed in the nineteenth century. Various progressive movements emerged and, as part of that shift in social thinking, people began to ask why it was acceptable to impose suffering on animals just because they were not rational, or self-aware, or otherwise like humans. For example, the English philosopher and lawyer Jeremy Bentham argued that although a full-grown horse or dog is more rational and more able to communicate than a human infant, "the question is not, Can they *reason?* nor, Can they *talk?* but, Can they *suffer?*" Humans and nonhumans may be different in many respects, but they are relevantly similar in that they are both sentient; they are percep-

tually aware and able to experience pain and pleasure. And there is no reason not to give weight to animal interests and, in particular, the interest in not suffering.

Did this mean that Bentham and others advocated that humans stop using animals for human purposes? Not at all. The fact that animals were supposedly not rational and otherwise had minds that were dissimilar to those of humans did not give humans a license to do whatever they wanted with animals, but it did mean that it was morally acceptable to use and kill them for human purposes as long as we treated them well. According to Bentham, animals live in the present and are not aware of what they lose when we take their lives. If we kill and eat them, "we are the better for it, and they are never the worse. They have none of those long-protracted anticipations of future misery which we have."

And thus was born the idea that animals do not, as a factual matter, have an interest in continuing to live, and death is not a harm for them. It's morally acceptable to use and kill animals as long as we minimize animal suffering. That moral sentiment was translated into laws that were enacted in Britain in the nineteenth century and then spread throughout much of the rest of the world, prohibiting humans from imposing "unnecessary" suffering on animals.

Although the idea that humans had the direct moral obligations to treat animals "humanely" represented a significant paradigm shift, it was, however, clear that this moral commitment remained woefully unfulfilled in most respects. During the nineteenth and twentieth centuries, the exploitation of animals got worse and not better.

In the 1970s, first in Britain, and then in the United States, a new group of progressives rediscovered what Bentham and others recognized two hundred years ago: animals were, in effect, being treated as though they were things that existed wholly outside the legal and moral community. Although there was important work done at this time before Peter Singer's entry on the scene, it was Singer's work that is regarded as the beginning of the "animal rights" era.

Although Singer, like Bentham, argues that we are not giving adequate weight to animal interests, he does not advocate that we stop using animals altogether. Like Bentham, Singer does not regard most animals as caring about *whether* we use them for our purposes but only about *how* we use them. They do not care whether they continue to exist because they are not self-aware, or capable of abstract thought. He states that "[a]n animal may struggle against a threat to its life, even if it cannot grasp that it has "a life" in the sense that requires an understanding of what it is to exist over a period of time. But in the absence of some form of mental continuity it is not easy to explain why the loss to the animal killed is not, from an impartial point of view, made good by the creation of a new animal who will lead an equally pleasant life."

Singer maintains that if we accord sufficient moral weight to animal interests in not suffering, we may continue to consume animals:

> If it is the infliction of suffering that we are concerned about, rather than killing, then I can also imagine a world in which people mostly eat plant foods, but occasionally treat themselves to the luxury of free range eggs, or possibly even meat from animals who live good lives under conditions natural for their species, and are then humanely killed on the farm.

Does the notion that animals do not have an interest in their lives, that they have an interest only in not suffering, make any sense?

I don't think so.

To say that a sentient being—any sentient being—is not harmed by death is most peculiar. Sentience is not a characteristic that has evolved to serve as an end in itself. Rather, it is a trait that allows beings to identify situations that are harmful and that threaten survival. *Sentience is a means to the end of continued existence.* Sentient beings, by virtue of their being sentient, have an interest in remaining alive; that is, they prefer, want or desire to remain alive. Therefore, to say that a sentient being is not harmed by death denies that the being has the very interest that sentience serves to perpetuate. It would be analogous to saying that a being with eyes does not have an interest in continuing to see or is not harmed by being made blind. The Jains of India expressed it well long ago: "All beings are fond of life, like pleasure, hate pain, shun destruction, like life, long to live. To all life is dear."

Singer recognizes that "[a]n animal may struggle against a threat to its life," but he denies that the animal has the mental continuity required for a morally significant sense of self. This position begs the question, however, in that it assumes that the only way that an animal can be self-aware is to have the sort of autobiographical sense of self that we associate with normal adult humans. That is certainly one way of being self-aware, but it is not the only way. As biologist Donald Griffin, one of the most important cognitive ethologists of the twentieth century, notes, if animals are conscious of anything, "the animal's own body and its own actions must fall within the scope of its perceptual consciousness." We nevertheless deny animals self-awareness because we maintain that they cannot "think such thoughts as 'It is *I* who am running, or climbing this tree, or chasing that moth.'" Griffin maintains that "when an animal consciously perceives the running, climbing, or moth-chasing of another animal, it must also be aware of who is doing these things. And if the animal is perceptually conscious of its own body, it is difficult to rule out similar recognition that it, itself, is doing the running, climbing, or chasing." He concludes that "[i]f animals are capable of perceptual awareness, denying them some level of self-awareness would seem to be an arbitrary and unjustified restriction."

It would seem that any sentient being must be self-aware, in that to be sentient means to be the sort of being who recognizes that she or he, and not some other, is experiencing pain or distress. When a sentient being is in pain, she necessarily recognizes that it is she who is in pain; there is some*one* who is conscious of being in pain and who has a preference, desire or want not to have that experience.

We can see the problematic nature of the Singer-Bentham position if we consider humans who have a condition known as transient global amnesia, which occurs as a result of a stroke, a seizure or brain damage. Those with transient global amnesia often have no memory of the past and no ability to project themselves into the future. These humans have, in the words of neuroscientist Antonio Damasio, "a sense of self about one moment—now—and about one place—here." Their sense of self-awareness may be different from that of a normal adult, but it would not be accurate to say that they are not self-aware or that they are indifferent to death. We may not want to appoint such a person as a teacher or allow her to perform surgery on others, but

most of us would be horrified at the suggestion that it is acceptable to use such people as forced organ donors or as non-consenting subjects in biomedical experiments, even if we did so "humanely."

Even if animals live in a similar "eternal present," that does not mean that they are not self-aware, that they have no morally significant interest in continued existence or that death does not harm them. A similar analysis holds for what Singer identifies as "any other capacity that could reasonably be said to give value to life." Some humans will not have the capacity at all, some will have it less than other humans and some will have it less than other nonhumans. This deficiency or difference may be relevant for some purposes, but it does not allow us to conclude that a human lacking the capacities that Singer identifies as giving value to life does not have an interest in continuing to live or that death does not harm her.

Do nonhuman animals have different minds from those of "normal" humans? Probably. We are the only animals who use symbolic communication so our minds are probably very different from the minds of beings who do not. But so what? To the extent that humans and nonhumans have different sorts of minds, those differences may be relevant for some purposes, just as differences between and among humans may be relevant for some purposes. Mary's greater ability at math may justify our giving her a scholarship over Joe, who lacks ability at math. Our four rescued dogs very much like to sit with us when we watch movies, but we do not consider their likes and dislikes in movies when we choose a movie because, at least as far as we can tell, they do not have any. There are relevant differences between the minds of humans and the minds of nonhumans. Any differences, however, are not logically relevant to, for instance, whether we use dogs in painful experiments or kill them for other purposes, just as Joe's inability to do math is not relevant to whether we should take his kidney to save Mary or use him in an experiment to obtain data that may benefit Mary.

To be clear: if a being is sentient—that is, if she is subjectively aware—then she has an interest in continuing to live, and death harms her. It is not necessary to have the autobiographical sense of self that we associate with normal adult humans. Moreover, we cannot say that her interests in her life or the quality of her pain or pleasure are of lesser moral value because her cognitions are not the same as those of normal adult humans. The fact that the minds of humans differ from nonhumans does not mean that the life of a human has greater moral value any more than it means that the life of a human who has normal mental capacities has greater moral value than the life of a mentally disabled person or that the life of an intelligent person has greater moral value than the life of a less intelligent one. Although the differences between humans and animals may be important for some purposes, they are completely irrelevant to the morality of using and killing animals, even if we do so "humanely."*

---

* I maintain that we cannot, as a practical matter, provide "humane" treatment to animals given that animals are property or economic commodities. Standards of animal welfare will necessarily be very low and, as a general matter, we protect animal interests only when we get an economic benefit from doing so. The goal of animal welfare is to ensure the economically efficient exploitation of animals and not to recognize any inherent value on the part of animals. For a discussion of this topic, see Gary L. Francione, *Animals as Persons: Essays on the Abolition of Animal Exploitation* (New York: Columbia University Press, 2008), 67-128. It is my view that animals have a moral right not to be treated as property. See ibid, at 25-66; Gary L. Francione, *Introduction to Ani-*

REJECTING OUR CONVENTIONAL WISDOM

The limited purpose of this essay was to explain how PETA *could* think it morally acceptable to kill animals and why PETA's thinking, which reflects Singer's thinking and is a version of our conventional wisdom, is just plain wrong.

The present debate on animal ethics in the United States, Great Britain and most Western countries focuses on whether we can morally justify raising animals in the crowded conditions known as "factory farming." But the debate takes that form because we focus on *treatment* and not on *use*. We focus on whether we can justify the suffering of animals raised for food. But we do not stop and think about whether the real issue is whether our use— *however* "humane" it may be—can be justified. And we don't think about that because we have accepted the idea that animals do not care about their lives.

Ironically, one of the reasons that so many of us reject PETA's killing of *any* healthy dogs and cats is that those of us who have lived with these animals recognize that is wrong to regard them as not having an interest in continued life. Our relationships with these animals allows us to see—clearly—that although the minds of these animals are different from the minds of humans, they are similar enough to justify our concluding that their untimely death is a tragedy, not just for us, but for them.

I suggest that rather than extending our conventional wisdom that death does not harm

---

mal Rights: Your Child or the Dog? (Philadelphia, Pa.: Temple University Press, 2000), 81-102.

an animal to cover dogs and cats, as PETA appears to do, we reject our conventional wisdom altogether and recognize that the only reason why we ever believed it wise in the first place was that we are desperate to find a justification that allows us to keep using animals for food and other purposes.

So my answer to the question put by *The Point*, "What are animals for?" is: animals are not for us to use, however "humanely."

USING ANIMALS

by Heather Keenleyside

This symposium opens with a provocation: What are animals for? The question almost solicits its own rejection, invoking as it does one of the central tenets of much animal advocacy: animals are not *for* anything, and they ought to be liberated from any sort of use. (Within animal ethics, the abolitionist or animal rights position is often distinguished from the animal welfare position, but both share the common and perhaps commonsensical thought that use is a problem; something that should be limited, curtailed or ended altogether.) This tenet finds one of its most pointed formulations in the work of legal scholar Gary Francione, who diagnoses contemporary Western culture with a "moral schizophrenia" about animals: "We treat some nonhumans as persons, as members of our families; we treat some as things that we eat or use in other ways." Behind Francione's charge of schizophrenia is something of a Kantian logic in which the ethical universe is carved into two: persons, ends-in-themselves that demand respect; and things, entities available as means, consigned to use. Francione puts this bluntly: "[Animals] are either persons, beings to whom the principle of equal consideration applies and who possess morally significant interests in not suffering, or things, beings to whom the principle of equal consideration does not apply and whose interests may be ignored if it benefits us. There is no third choice."

I want to think a bit more about the two choices Francione lays out—either persons or things, either ethical consideration or use. I want to think, in particular, about use. Many people concerned with the ethics of human-animal relations share Francione's sense that use is a problem. In the introduction to the 1983 anthology, *Ethics and Animals*, for example, we find a section entitled "Using the Others," along with the following list: "We use other animals in many ways: we eat them, experiment upon them, test an enormous number of substances on them, hunt and kill them for entertainment, race and fight them for entertainment, produce a wide variety of products from the uneaten parts of their bodies, and keep them as pets and as servants." Later in the same volume, Annette Baier glosses the standard (Kantian) thought "that it is only right and proper that [animals] serve the ends of rational beings like us, thus becoming our food, our clothing, our playthings, our prey, our experimental subjects our guinea-pigs, and our sacrificial lambs." In each case, the form of the list implies a kind of equivalence between different sorts of use—the use of animals as food and as entertainment, as prey and as plaything. This is a familiar move, but I'm not sure it's a self-evident one.

In looking for the logic that underwrites this equation of different sorts of use, we could do worse than turn to Locke's *Two Treatises of Government*, a foundational text for our notion of what it means to treat something as a thing, as something available for use. In developing his account of the origin of our right to use things—of the ground of property rights—Locke bypasses the text to which many before and after him have turned: the first chapter of Genesis, in which God grants Adam (and humankind) dominion over all creatures. "Let them have dominion over the fish of the sea, and over the fowl of the air, and over the cattle, and over all the earth, and over every creeping thing that creepeth upon the earth." For

Katie Kline, *Anaheim*, 2005

reasons of his own—which have to do with distinguishing private property from property in common, as well as with extending private property to an unprecedented degree—Locke isn't satisfied with Adam's dominion. He is interested instead in God's covenant with Noah some nine chapters later. For only then, as Locke writes, did Noah and his sons have "given them the utmost Property Man is capable of, which is to have a right to destroy any thing by using it; *Every moving thing that Liveth*, saith God, *shall be Meat for you*, which was not allowed to *Adam* in his Charter." (Adam was granted, as Locke notes, "the Herbs but in common with the Beasts"). Noah's "right to destroy any thing by using it"—that is, his right to eat animals, to use moving, living things as food—is for Locke the origin and the paradigm of private property. And it seems to me that we can see something of a Lockean logic (though it is not Locke's alone) in our common notions of what it is to use: to use is to use up or to destroy, on the paradigm, here, of eating animals.

There may be conceptual and strategic gains to be had from equating use with using up, on the model of eating. But I think there are also losses. I think of Barbara Johnson's recent reflections on "the ethical importance of 'using people,'" for example, which reads Kant with the psychoanalyst Donald Winnicott to defend a particular kind of use—the way an infant uses her first possession or her mother—as crucial to living well with others. This may seem a long way from the sort of use that concerns animals, and it is. But as Johnson's Winnicottian sense of use opens onto the scene or subject of play, it also recalls Montaigne's question about using animals as playthings, which undercuts any sense that use goes only one way: "When I am playing with my cat, how do I know she is not playing with me?" In a very different register, I also think of

Porphyry's *On Abstinence from Animal Food*, one of the most important classical discussions of animal ethics, which insists on distinguishing "laborious uses" like shearing sheep, milking cows, taming and yoking oxen, from the use of animals for food. Each of these examples makes a similar point: not all use is equal. And each makes a case, too, that use is not necessarily anathema to ethical consideration, as it is for animal rights advocates like Francione.

In Porphyry, social and ethical relations often go together with relations of use, and sometimes stem from them. Porphyry insists that we owe justice above all to the animals with whom we associate most closely, and of which we make use: "The ox that ploughs, the dog that is fed with us, and the animals that nourish us with their milk, and adorn our bodies with their wool." Henry Salt says something similar in his landmark 1892 defense, *Animal Rights: Considered in Relation to Social Progress*, namely that the animals we use "have a special claim on man's courtesy and sense of fairness, inasmuch as they are not his fellow-creatures only, but his fellow-workers, his dependents, and in many cases the familiar associates and trusted inmates of his home." These may sound like sentimental and perhaps wrongheaded efforts to satisfy the demands of justice with something like benevolence or kindness. They may, in part, be that. And yet our ways of living with animals would be radically transformed if we took seriously the sorts of ethical obligations that Salt and Porphyry think stem from all that animals are for.

To set use and association together as Salt and Porphyry do is to move into the domestic realm, where humans and animals have long lived (and worked and played) together. Among those who think and write about animals, philosopher Mary Midgley has paid particular attention to this domestic realm.

Reminding us that no other species "draw[s] in, domesticate[s] and live[s] with a great variety of other creatures ... on anything like so large a scale," Midgley urges us to "take this peculiar human talent more seriously and try to understand its workings." To think seriously about domestication would, I think, make it difficult to divide the world into persons and things, or to identify use with using up. We might instead see a world in which it is difficult to parse person from thing, family from food, companion from property. Midgley's word for this is "association": her examples include dogs (animals "with whom our association seems to be an incredibly ancient one, amounting to symbiosis"), but also reindeer, weasels and elephants, the cattle of the Masai and the horses of nomads. All of these associations are explicitly social relations and also relations of use; in each case, as Midgley puts it, "tractors cannot be substituted." It's worth quoting Midgley at length here:

> Of course [domestic animals] were largely there for use—for draught and riding, for meat, milk, wool and hides, for feathers and eggs, as vermin-catchers or as aids to fishing or hunting. In principle, it might seem reasonable to expect that these forms of exploitation would have produced no personal or emotional involvement at all. From a position of ignorance, we might have expected that people would view their animals simply as machines. If we impose the sharp Kantian dichotomy between *persons* and *things*, subjects and objects, and insist that everything must be considered as simply one or the other, we might have expected that they would be viewed unambiguously as things. But in fact, if people had viewed them like

this, the domestication could probably never have worked. The animals, with the best will in the world, could not have reacted like machines. They became tame, not just through the fear of violence, but because they were able to form individual bonds with those who tamed them by coming to understand the social signals addressed to them. They learned to obey human beings personally. They were able to do this, not only because the people taming them were social beings, but because they themselves were so too. ... It is hopeless trying to understand this situation if we keep pressing the crude Kantian question, 'but are lambs people or things?' If we want to grasp it, we must wake up to a much wider range of possibilities. Our conceptual map needs revising.

For Midgley, revising our conceptual map means that there is indeed a third choice between Francione's respect for persons and the use, as using up, of things: a position occupied by domestic animals and our associations with them. For Johnson, revising our conceptual map means crossing Francione's two choices to think more about the ways in which persons are treated as things (and things as persons), as well as the ways in which use might be an ethical good. In both cases, it is the domestic realm that prompts or requires this kind of conceptual revision. Domestic relations (between an infant and her first possession, between a nomad and his horse) call for ethical paradigms that are sensitive to conditions of dependence, vulnerability and embodied life, to scenes of work and play as well as of potentially nondestructive, even ethical forms of use.

•

I've been arguing that those of us concerned with animals might do well to consider use outside of the paradigm of using up, destruction or eating. What, then, about eating? Is there a way to bring eating into the field of ethics—to take not only the nomad and the horse as a model of moral relation, but also the eater and the eaten? I admit I'm not sure. To borrow a phrase from Baier, "the moral enterprise is built on the faith that interests can to some extent be reconciled, that flourishing need not always be at the expense of others." And eating, by definition, would seem to be flourishing at the expense of others. But eating also raises questions about what counts as a unit of flourishing, and so troubles ethics in part by troubling boundaries between individuals. One doesn't have to think for long about eating before one comes to the idea of the food chain, which is not so much a model of one individual flourishing at the expense of others as it is one in which individuals are difficult to discern at all. Porphyry criticizes the Stoic philosopher Chrysippus for invoking the food chain to underwrite his extreme formulation of the claim "that animals are for man," which holds together various sorts of use: bugs are for waking us up, mice are for making us put away our things, pigs are for eating. Porphyry replies that "if we define, by utility, things which pertain to us, we shall not be prevented from admitting, that we were generated for the sake of the most destructive animals, such as crocodiles, balaenae, and dragons." I find Porphyry's move (like Chrysippus') striking for the way it can seem at once true and trite, the way it can induce a sense of both vertigo and banality. It can do this, I think, because it rests on what is finally a formal and reversible ecological point, that all is interconnected: pigs are useful to man, man is useful to crocodiles. This point says little about how to move from ecology to ethics, from the food chain to individual units of concern or value, from the fact of interdependence to the normative sense of being "for." It says little about how we might decide who or what is to be used by whom, and how.

In his captivating work of environmental legal theory, *Should Trees Have Standing*, Christopher Stone argues that taking the ecological fact of interdependence seriously unsettles the sense that anything—person, animal or thing—is "for" anything else. Stone insists that nothing that exists is simply given for human flourishing or food or use:

> To be able to get away from the view that Nature is a collection of useful senseless objects is ... to reach a heightened awareness of our own, and others', capacities in mutual interplay. To do so, we have to give up some psychic investment in our sense of separateness and specialness in the universe. And this, in turn, is hard giving indeed, because it involves us in a flight backwards, into earlier stages of civilization and childhood in which we had to trust (and perhaps fear) our environment, for we had not then the power to master it. Yet, in doing so, we, as persons, gradually free ourselves of needs for supportive illusions.

Stone doesn't specify what supportive illusions we might get free of if we as a species were to return to something like childhood.

But I take it that the separateness or special-ness that we might give up is that of the human species, but also that of individual persons, and, perhaps, of individual animals as well.

The relationship between animal rights and environmentalism is often uneasy, not least because animal rights tends to worry about individual animals, while much of en-vironmental thought moves toward ecological units like species, ecosystems and the food chain. For those interested in ethics and ani-mals, there is often a sense that the individual animal (like the individual person) is some-thing separate and special in the universe, something given for our concern or respect, something that demands freedom from being used, or at least from being used up. There are good reasons for this sense, including notions of what it means to be alive or have a life, to suffer or be free from pain, to be endowed with consciousness, sentience or feeling. But I won-der whether something might not be gained from starting at the other end, with things. Per-haps thinking environmentalism and animal rights together—thinking ethics in ways that might encompass humans and animals and also Stone's trees—requires us to think more capaciously about use, but also to acknowledge that carving out units of concern or respect is difficult and often uncertain work. We (hu-mans, persons) are not separate and special in the universe, though we can be. So too can others, animals and things alike. I am attracted to Porphyry's defense of vegetarianism, which he frames as an injunction against treating animals as things: "For how is it possible that he should not defame and calumniate animals, who has determined to cut them in pieces, as if they were stones." Instinctively, I sense that it is a defamation of animals to treat them as if they were stones. But then maybe we need to think more about how we treat stones.

GETTING ANIMALS IN VIEW

by Christine M. Korsgaard

What sorts of philosophical problems do we face because of the existence of non-human animals? Most humane people would agree that their existence presents us with some moral and legal quandaries. And recently, but only recently, philosophers have taken a serious interest in the character of animal minds. But I have come to think that animals present us with a philosophical problem deeper than either of those—that the existence of non-human animals is the source of a profound disturbance in the way that human beings conceptualize the world. It is almost as if we—I'm using "we" to mean "us human beings" here—are unable to get them firmly into view, to see them for what they really are.

Many people, to take one small example, find nothing odd about the sentence, "I live alone with a cat." Okay, granted, someone might also say, "I live alone with a child," at least so long as the child was a very small one.* But "I live alone with four children" would be

starting to put the language under stress, even if they were all toddlers, while "I live alone with four cats" would not. Here's another example: People wondering about whether there might be life on other planets sometimes ask, "Are we alone in the universe?" Just look around! Well, you may reply, they mean to ask whether there is any other *intelligent* life in the universe. Right. Just look around!

Animals also seem to pop in and out of our moral view. Most people would agree that it is wrong to hurt or kill a non-human animal without a good reason, but then it turns out that any reason, short of malicious pleasure, is reason enough. We want to eat the animal, and to raise her cheaply for that purpose; we can learn from doing experiments on her; we can make useful or attractive products out of her; she is interfering with our agriculture or gardening; or maybe we just don't feel comfortable having her come so near. Her interests have weight, we insist—but never weight enough to outweigh our own.

Then there is the disturbing use of the phrase "treated like an animal." People whose rights are violated, people whose interests are ignored or overridden, people who are used, harmed, neglected, starved or unjustly imprisoned standardly complain that they are being treated like animals, or protest that after all they are not just animals. Of course, rhetorically, complaining that you are being treated like an animal is more effective than complaining that you are being treated like a thing or an object or a stone, for a thing or an object or a stone has no interests that can be ignored or overridden. In the sense intended, an object *can't* be treated badly, while an animal can. But then the curious implication seems to be that animals are the beings that it's all right to treat badly, and the complainant is saying that he is not one of *those*.

---

* There's interference here from another use of "I live alone with" in which it means, "I have sole charge of": "I can't go out whenever I please; I live alone with the an autistic child." That's obviously not what is meant by "I live alone with a cat," but it might be what's meant by "I live alone with a child." But notice that very small babies, like animals, get called "it." It's tempting to speculate that this practice dates from the days when human infant mortality rates were higher and babies, like non-human animals, were regarded as fungible.

Katie Kline, *Galveston*, 2011

Do we need that contrast, between the beings it is *all right* to treat badly and the ones it is not? My otherwise favorite philosopher, Immanuel Kant, seemed to think so. In his essay "Conjectures on the Beginning of Human History," Kant traces the development of reason through a series of steps, the last of which is this:

> The fourth and last step which reason took, thereby raising man completely above animal society, was his ... realization that he is the true *end of nature* ... When he first said to the sheep 'the pelt which you wear was given to you by nature not for your own use, but for mine' and took it from the sheep to wear it himself, he became aware of a prerogative which ... he enjoyed over all the animals; and he now no longer regarded them as fellow creatures, but as means and instruments to be used at will for the attainment of whatever ends he pleased. This notion implies ... an awareness of the following distinction: man should not address other *human beings* in the same way as animals, but should regard them as having an equal share in the gifts of nature. ... Thus man had attained a position of *equality with all rational beings*, because he could claim *to be an end in himself* ... and not to be used by anyone else as a mere means to other ends.

Non-human animals, on this showing, are the ultimate and final Other. They are the beings we can still use as mere means once we have given up the idea that other human beings are there for our purposes—once we've rejected the ideas that women are *for* housework and childcare, that girls are *for* sex, that boys are *for* fighting wars that serve older men's interests, and that people of color are *for* harvesting the fields and doing the menial jobs that all of us hate. Is that, to revert to this symposium's theme, what animals are for? Are they there so that there will be someone we can still use as mere means to our ends?

Not being what Kant called a "mere means" is not a privative condition—a way of being useless, say. It's a positive condition, which Kant calls being an "end in yourself." For a human being, it means that your choices should be respected and your ends promoted, that you have rights that the community should be prepared to uphold, that your happiness is valuable and your suffering should be cured or mitigated or met with tenderness when it is beyond cure. "Morality" is our name for demanding this kind of treatment from one another, and for meeting that demand. When we do use others to serve our own purposes— for of course we do—it must be done in a way that is consistent with all this, and then we are not treating them as "mere means," but at the same time as ends in themselves. But why shouldn't the other animals also be treated as ends in themselves?

I'll come back to that question. But first, let me respond to those readers who are now tempted to protest that there are plenty of people who *do* treat the other animals as ends in themselves. After all, it is notorious these days that more people than ever not only live with companion animals, but treat them like human children, keeping them in the house, providing them with toys and furniture, buying them medical insurance, bribing their affection with treats and burying them in graveyards when they die. Of course it's also true that in tough economic times when there is no longer money for such indulgences, these companion animals are turned loose onto the streets and into shelters in a way that human children ordinarily are not. But even those of us who are convinced that *we* would never treat our beloved pets in this way should remember that keeping an animal for affection and companionship is also a way of *using* the animal. Is it using the animal as a "mere means"?

It could be. Even among people, of course, it is possible to use someone for affection and companionship without keeping her existence and value as an independent being firmly in view. In *Middlemarch*, George Eliot tells the story of Dorothea, an idealistic young woman hungry to do some good in the world, who marries an older man whom she conceives to be a scholar engaged in a great work. Eliot writes:

> We are all of us born in moral stupidity, taking the world as an udder to feed our supreme selves: Dorothea had early begun to emerge from that stupidity, but yet it had been easier to her to imagine how she would devote herself to Mr. Casaubon, and become wise and strong in his strength and wisdom, than to conceive with that distinctness which is no longer reflection but feeling—an idea wrought back to the directness of sense, like the solidity of objects—that he had an equivalent center of self, whence the lights and shadows must always fall with a certain difference.

Eliot's purpose, at the particular moment at which this passage occurs, is to emphasize that Dorothea has failed to understand Casaubon's feelings. She has not quite managed to get his "center of self" into her view. But the moment is also one of moral revelation, a moment in which Dorothea grasps that "there is as great a need on his side as on her own" and so acquires "a new motive." Eliot is accusing her heroine,

just a little, of having used Casaubon as a mere means to give significance and purpose to her own life. How much easier, then, to do something like that to a creature whose "center of self" you may not—rightly or wrongly—grant to be the "equivalent" of your own.

Is it because the other animals have lesser "centers of self" that so many people suppose they are not entitled to be treated as ends in themselves? In his Tanner Lectures, written as a work of fiction called *The Lives of Animals*, J. M. Coetzee imagines a professional philosopher who says: "It is licit to kill animals because their lives are not as important to them as ours are to us." George Eliot reminds us how hard it is to keep in view—not just to tell yourself, but to feel with "the directness of sense"—that other *people's* lives are as just important to them as yours is to you. But we are at least theoretically committed to the importance, and the equal importance, of every human life. Many of our religious and philosophical traditions try to explain this equal importance. We, these traditions assert—we human beings, that is—are all God's children, or have some special sort of intrinsic value that the other animals lack. But what makes it possible to believe such things at all is probably the thing that Coetzee puts in his philosopher's mouth: the passionate sense of importance that each of us attaches to himself or herself. After all, every human being pursues the things that are important to himself and to those whom he loves as if they were important *absolutely*, important in deadly earnest—for what else can we do? And just by doing that, we claim our own standing as ends in ourselves. For when we claim that the things that are important to us should be treated as important absolutely, just because they are important to us, we also claim that we are important ourselves.* But the other animals also pursue the things that are important to them and their loved ones as if they were important in deadly earnest. Why then should we think they must be less important to themselves than we are to ourselves?

Some of the philosophical views about the nature of animal minds are, among other things, attempts to answer that question. The other animals are not conscious at all, some people argue, or their consciousness is so fleeting and ephemeral that it just does not add up to the consciousness of a self, so nothing really could matter to them in quite the same that way it does to us. A less extreme version of that last view—one that even many defenders of the moral claims of animals, such as Peter Singer, endorse—is that animals live so thoroughly in the moment that their deaths are not regrettable, although their suffering is.

That might seem puzzling. After all, when we consider our fellow human beings, we often regard a capacity for living in the moment as a good thing. The human mind can be so cluttered and overshadowed with worries about the future and regrets about the past that we fail to enjoy the present—the only thing, after all, that is real. So why would the fact that the other animals live in the moment, supposing it is a fact, make their deaths less regrettable? Jeff MacMahan offers this explanation:

> ... the lives of persons typically have a narrative structure that may demand completion in a certain way. People autonomously establish purposes for their lives, form patterns of structured relations with oth-

ers, and thereby create expectations and dependencies that require fulfillment. The importance of later events in a typical human life may thus be greatly magnified by their relation to ambitions formed and activities engaged in earlier ... In the lives of animals, however, this potential for complex narrative unity is entirely absent. There are no projects that require completion, mistakes that demand rectification, or personal relations that promise to ripen or mature. Rather, as Aldous Huxley once put it, "the dumb creation lives a life made up of discreet and mutually irrelevant episodes." And each day is merely more of the same.

According to this argument, to deprive a human being of life is worse than to deprive another animal of life, because you are depriving the non-human animal only of "more of the same," while you may be disrupting the narrative unity of the human being's life.

I have mixed reactions to this kind of argument. On the one hand, animal lives are not the same every day—rather, at least for many of them, they have a rhythm that is set by the seasons of the year, and by the age of breeding, and may involve the raising of families, migrations, the building of homes, preparation for the winter and so on. Many mother animals raise new young every year or so, and most of those die and presumably are forgotten, but in some social animals, the bonds that result from family ties are permanent and important. Relationships, families and larger social groups persist over time. For some animals there is even a narrative structure to the course of an individual life that *we* can recognize and describe—even if they cannot. Among social animals, for instance, certain male individuals rise to positions of power and leadership

---

* These remarks are a loose reading of Kant's claim that "representing" ourselves as ends in ourselves is a subjective principle of human action. See *Groundwork of the Metaphysics of Morals*, 4:429.

in middle age, only to be deposed by younger members when they are older. Females move through a distinct set of roles in family life as daughters, then mothers, then grandmothers in much the same way that, in many cultures, human females do.

Which brings me to the other side of what bothers me about this—that human lives also have established rhythms set by the seasons of the year and the age of breeding, and that many human lives, especially when you look at the species historically, or at less developed nations, have been pretty much the same every day. You get up, do some work, eat breakfast, then do some more work. You tend the children and prepare the food, or you feed the animals, or you hoe the fields, or you go to the factory, depending on when and where your life takes place, but you go to work, and then you have supper, and then go to bed and start over. Each day is merely more of the same. Perhaps it is exactly those lives that most challenge the ability of the more privileged members of developed nations to feel with "the directness of sense" that every person's life is just as important to her as ours are to us.

Yet there is clearly something right about MacMahan's picture. I think it is this: we human beings, unlike the other animals, think of ourselves and our lives in normative terms. We are governed not merely by instinctive likes and dislikes, attractions and aversions, enjoyment and suffering, but by values. Being reflective animals, we endorse or reject our likes and dislikes, attractions and aversions, pleasures or pains, declaring them to be good or bad. Each of us identifies himself in terms of certain roles, relationships, occupations and causes, all of them governed by normative standards, which it is then the business of our lives to live up to. And so we come to think of ourselves as worthy or unworthy, lovable or unlovely, good or bad.

Philosophers disagree about what exactly it is about our nature that makes us like this—whether it is rationality, or a special kind of sentiment, or something else. However that may be, this kind of evaluative self-conception is a condition that gives a strange extra dimension to human life, both a special source of pride and interest, and a profound cause of suffering. It is not that nothing is important to the other animals, for instinctive desire and aversion have an imperative character all their own. But that does not seem to suffuse whatever sense of their own being the other animals have. Some of the other animals seem to have moments of pride, but they don't seem in general to think of themselves as worthy or unworthy beings. Some of them certainly want to be loved, but they don't seem to worry about being lovable. Thinking of yourself as having a kind of identity that is at once up to you and subject to normative assessment is a distinctive feature of being human. It gives a human being's life, in his own eyes, the character of a *project*, of something at which he can succeed or fail. That possibility of success or failure is what gives human life the kind of narrative structure that MacMahan describes.

If this is right, it shows that human lives are important to human beings in *a way* that the lives of the other animals are not important to them. But it does not show that our lives are *more* important than theirs. It is not that our lives have a kind of importance that the lives of the other animals lack. It is rather that our lives have a kind of importance *for us* that the other animals' lives do not have *for them*. And I am prepared to make a further claim here: that there is nothing that is therefore *missing* from the lives of the other animals.

This is where things start to get a little bit dizzying, conceptually speaking. The difficulty is that everything that is important must be important because it is important *to* someone: to some person or animal. What makes it important to that person or animal is that it satisfies some desire or conforms to some standard that applies to that person or animal. But the standard of normative success and failure, which goes with the project of making yourself into a worthy or an unworthy being, does not apply to the other animals. There is nothing missing from the lives of the other animals because they fail to see themselves as good or bad, successes or failures. The standards that we use when we measure ourselves in these ways apply to us in virtue of something about our nature, and do not apply to them.

Perhaps a comparison will help. John Stuart Mill famously claimed that it is better to be Socrates dissatisfied than a pig satisfied.* Mill believed this because he held that human beings have access to what he called "higher pleasures"—for instance, the pleasures of poetry. But for whom is it better? Would it be better *for the pig* if he were Socrates? Temple Grandin, in her book *Animals Make Us Human*, reports that there is nothing pigs love more than rooting around in straw. Poetry is not good for a pig, so it is not something valuable that is missing from the pig's life, something he would get access to if he were changed into Socrates, any more than rooting around in straw is something valuable that is missing from your life, something you would get access to if you were changed into a pig. But isn't poetry a higher pleasure than rooting around in straw? If what makes a pleasure "higher" is, as Kant and others have suggested, that it cultivates our capacity for even deeper and greater pleasures

of the very same kind, then we must have that capacity before the pleasure can be judged a higher one for us. Since the pig lacks that capacity, poetry is not a higher pleasure for a pig. Of course, we might try the argument that, so far as we can tell, none of the pig's pleasures are "higher" in this sense. But then perhaps it is only for us jaded human beings that the lower pleasures seem to grow stale. So long as the straw itself is fresh, pigs apparently *never* lose their enthusiasm for rooting around in straw.

There's a notorious philosophical problem about thoughts that begin, "if I were you..." When I tell you what I would do if I were you, I must bring something of myself with me, usually some standard for the assessment of actions that also applies to you, or a superior ability to apply some standard that we already share. Otherwise it's a foregone conclusion that whatever *you* would do if I weren't offering you advice is exactly what I would do if I were you. But the standard I bring with me may be one that does not apply to you or that you do not share. David Hume reminds us of the famous story of the advice Parmenio gave to Alexander the Great. *"Were I Alexander,* said Parmenio, *I would accept of these offers made by Darius. So would I too,* replied Alexander, *were I Parmenio."* This problem pervades our efforts to think about the other animals, for when we try to think about what it is like to be another animal, we bring our human standards with us, and then the other animals seem to us like lesser beings. A human being who lives a life governed only by desires and instincts, not by values, would certainly be a lesser being. But that doesn't mean that the other animals are lesser beings. They are simply beings of a different kind. When we look at the other animals through the lens of our own standards, just as when we look at them through the lens of our own interests, we cannot get them properly in view.

---

* Actually Mill claims, on p. 10 of *Utilitarianism*, that it is better to be a human being dissatisfied than a pig satisfied, and better to be Socrates dissatisfied than a fool satisfied, so I am merging his claims by taking Socrates as the exemplar of humanity here.

We are all born, as Eliot says, in moral stupidity, unable to see others except through the lens of our own interests and standards. Kant suggested that it took four steps for us to emerge from this moral stupidity, but perhaps there is a fifth step we have yet to take. That is to try to look at the other animals and their lives unhindered by our own interests and specifically human standards, and to see them for what they really are. What is important about the other animals is what we have in common: that they, like us, are the kinds of beings to whom things *can* be important. Like us, they pursue the things that are important *to* them as if they were important *absolutely*, important in deadly earnest—for, like us, what else can they do? When we do this, we claim our own standing as ends in ourselves. But our only reason for doing that is that it is essential to the kinds of beings we are, beings who take their own concerns to be important. The claim of the other animals to the standing of ends in themselves has same ultimate foundation as our own—the essentially self-affirming nature of life itself.

IMAGINATION AND ADVOCACY

by Alice Crary

Works of art that engage us, directing our sense of what is important and inviting us to see the world in a new way, are sometimes described as appealing to "moral imagination." These works are often employed in animal advocacy, yet they present something of a mystery from a philosophical perspective. Documentaries, for example, clearly impart information. But something would be lost if they simply presented the bare facts like a lecture. The puzzle concerns the nature of this artistic remainder, this appeal to our imagination. Does it *merely* shape our feelings, or can it as such give insight into the way things actually are?

Take James Marsh's 2011 film *Project Nim*, which concerns the extraordinary life of a particular chimpanzee. Born in 1973 at the Oklahoma Institute for Primate Studies, the newborn Nim was taken from his mother and loaned out to a Columbia University psychology professor, Herbert Terrace, who hoped to demonstrate that chimps' capacity for learning human sign language was greater than generally believed. For nearly five years Nim lived in different human households, and during this period he was treated like a human child and taught to use many signs. But when Nim bit and badly injured one of his student handlers, Terrace unceremoniously deposited him back at the Oklahoma Institute for Primate Studies. Thanks to the care and attention of a research student named Bob Ingersoll, Nim, who had never before seen a member of his own species, eventually adjusted to life with other chimps. This was not, however, the end of his troubles. A few years after Nim's return all of the Institute's chimps were sold to the NYU Laboratory for Experimental Medicine and Surgery in Primates (LEMSIP) where, among other things, they were used to test vaccines for humans. Ingersoll worked hard to publicize Nim's plight, and eventually Nim was moved to an animal sanctuary in Texas called the Black Beauty Ranch. There Nim was given a relatively large concrete compound with a porch, but he lived alone. Ingersoll intervened again and arranged for two other chimps to move in with Nim. These chimps were Nim's companions for five years until his death in 2000.

The film that Marsh made about Nim deals with these and other events in Nim's life. Marsh made *Project Nim* because he wanted to understand the life of a particular chimp. But he didn't limit himself to the plain recital and visual presentation of facts. He does rely heavily on archival material such as movies and photographs taken by people who knew Nim. At the same time, he employs various methods that invite us to enter into and explore different perspectives on what happened to Nim. He employs images from the archival material in an expressive manner; he stages and films a number of reenactments, using them in a similarly evocative style; he adds his own formal interviews with some of the individuals who interacted most closely with Nim; and he uses music to capture the most psychologically and emotionally salient aspects of Nim's story. These different techniques shape our attitudes, inviting us to place importance on particular aspects of Nim's life, and a good case can be made for saying that they are essential to Marsh's goal of conveying an understanding of what that life was like.

Katie Kline, *London*, 2005

Consider how the film brings out the magnitude of the wrong that was done to Nim and the other chimps when they were sold to LEMSIP and used for testing vaccines. Relevant here are not only the parts of the film that are specifically concerned with LEMSIP but also the parts that show Nim in happy times. Some of Nim's happy times were at the Institute for Primate Studies. During the day he and his friends had access to an indoor compound with toys and climbing surfaces, and Nim himself also had Ingersoll, who took him for walks, roughhousing and simply hanging out with him. In one sequence, we see Ingersoll and Nim heading out of the compound, signing to each other in a relaxed manner. Ingersoll signs "where?" to Nim, and Nim responds by making the sign for "walk." Nim turns to Ingersoll, makes the sign for "play" and sprints energetically off across a field. As we see these images, Ingersoll tells us: "Chimps aren't humans. You have to kind of understand chimps to be able to ... work with them and be with them." We also hear a folksy musical phrase played repeatedly on an acoustic guitar, a melodic fragment that differs notably from the menacing riff that shows up when Nim is living with humans and threatening physical violence. The different techniques Marsh uses to show us Nim's life with Ingersoll thus position us to look at Nim's gestures and antics in an ethically non-neutral manner, so that we see in them the pulse of flourishing chimpanzee life and perceive in them a kind of vital glory.

These happy days form the background to Nim's time at LEMSIP, where individual chimpanzees are separated from each other and confined to small barren cages. Traumatized by what was done to them, they appear alternately groggy and frenzied. A veterinarian from LEMSIP explains that since he and his colleagues knew that some of the chimps could sign they posted pieces of paper with pictures of signs so that everyone in the lab could learn them. As this vet is speaking, the camera turns and—in what is evidently a re-enactment—scans a series of pieces of paper with drawings of signs on them, coming to rest briefly on a drawing of the sign for "hug" and then, after a brief interval, lingering on a drawing of the sign for "play." It is in this way—by means of a series of expressive techniques—that *Project Nim* conveys an understanding of the awfulness of what happened to Nim at LEMSIP. And what is impressed on us is a contrast with Nim's former life that could not be more poignant: however much the lab workers may want to sign meaningfully about hugging and playing with their chimp subjects, the magnificent chimp form of life to which hugging and playing belong has already been cruelly extinguished.

•

Do Marsh's expressive techniques contribute directly to ethical understanding of Nim's life? Might they, or something like them, even be *necessary* for such understanding? It might seem unlikely that moral imagination could have such power. As well-educated people alive in the twenty-first century, most of us believe that human beings are at bottom a kind of animal and that, like other animals, we are essentially subject to the conditions of physical existence. There is nothing about this image, considered by itself, that obliges us to deny that moral imagination is essential for understanding our worldly lives or the worldly lives of other animals. But when, in thinking about the ways in which humans and animals are natural creatures, we wax philosophical, we frequently assume that the natural world is ethically neutral or, to use a bit of philosophical jargon, "hard." And this seems to rule out the possibility that moral imagination might be required to illuminate aspects of this world and of the creatures that inhabit it.

However appealing this "hard" outlook may be in general, it is harmful for those who want to advocate on behalf of animals. Animal advocates want to show that animals merit certain forms of treatment *in themselves*, rather than in ways that are functions of treatment owed to human beings—and that, say, tying a hedgehog up in a ball and playing croquet with it on my lawn, as a fictional Alice once did, is an abuse in itself, regardless of whether it hurts or offends humans. It is very difficult to defend this view this while maintaining that the natural world has value only insofar as we project value onto it. Yet many animal advocates attempt just this feat.

Some of the most prominent, such as Peter Singer, Tom Regan, James Rachels and Jeff McMahan, flag their exclusive reliance on "hard" concepts of human beings and animals by declaring that, as they see it, the mere fact of being a human or an animal is by itself ethically unimportant. Singer and the others tell us that what makes a human or an animal deserving of moral consideration is its possession of certain individual capacities. While these thinkers disagree about which capacities are morally relevant—the capacity to suffer and the capacity to direct one's own life are the leading candidates—they all claim that, if we take a given capacity to be morally significant in human beings, consistency obliges us to treat it as morally significant in whichever animals also possess it. And then they claim that there are no morally significant capacities that

are possessed by all humans and no animals. This is indeed a strategy for showing that *some* animals matter. But it has famously disturbing consequences that speak strongly against it. It implies, for example, that severely retarded and extremely senile human beings have diminished claims to consideration and that mocking or abusing them isn't all that bad.

Singer and company aren't the only animal advocates who limit themselves to hard concepts of human beings and animals. A second group is an idiosyncratic collection of Kantian moral philosophers, the most prominent of whom is Christine Korsgaard. Korsgaard combats Kant's notoriously indifferent attitude toward animals with ideas found elsewhere in his thought. Kant's official view was that animals are mere things and that we should treat them well not because we owe it to them but because we owe it to our own moral characters. There isn't anything terribly striking about the fact that Korsgaard challenges this view, for so do Singer et al. What is striking is the fact that, when Korsgaard challenges the view, she claims that the plain recognition that a creature is a human or an animal (i.e. independently of any thought about its individual capacities) is inseparable from seeing it as meriting forms of respect and attention. Because Korsgaard makes this claim her work doesn't have the disturbing consequences that moral individualisms do. But the claim might appear to commit her to concepts of human beings and animals that are "non-hard" in the sense of being incompatible with an understanding of the world as ethically neutral. After all, how could we represent merely being a human, or merely being an animal, as ethically important without assuming that human beings and animals are intrinsically ethically significant things?

Korsgaard gives the following answer to this question. She insists that to recognize a creature as an animal or a human being is to adopt an exclusively *practical* attitude. This strategy allows her to depict animals as ethically interesting things—things that matter—while preserving an image of them as inhabitants of a hard world. And insofar as Korsgaard preserves this image, she limits herself to hard concepts of human beings and animals. So, like Singer, she is committed to a restrictive view of the methods appropriate to illuminating humans' and animals' worldly lives in ethics, specifically, one that cannot give moral imagination an essential role. And this constrains her ability to advocate on behalf of animals.

Why do animal advocates tend to equate "natural" with "ethically neutral"? Some help themselves to an understanding of the natural world as hard, together with all that goes with such an understanding, without registering the fact that they are thereby adopting a substantial philosophical position. But there are also animal advocates—such as Singer and Korsgaard—who are self-conscious about adopting hard metaphysical postures. Yet even these thinkers feel no need to explicitly defend their outlooks. One possible explanation is the assumption, widespread among philosophers, that to give up the idea of a hard world is to give up the idea of a world that is objective and that can support the idea of truth and falsity.

This assumption may seem to receive a sort of confirmation in the writings of Jacques Derrida, one of the most prominent contemporary European philosophers to discuss the lives of animals. Derrida wrote a great deal about animals during the last years of his life, and he consistently oriented his remarks by referring to passages in his early publications in which he attacks an understanding of the world as hard. He also consistently suggested that if we abandon such an understanding, as he thought we should, we thereby abandon the idea of full-blooded objectivity. He thus in effect defended the assumption, also cherished by many philosophers who are fans of a hard metaphysic, that the only alternative to a hard vision of the world is some sort of skepticism about objectivity.

But this assumption is false. To say that the natural world is hard is to commit oneself to speaking of nature only in reference to the subject matter of natural-scientific and other ethically neutral disciplines. There is, however, room for intelligent philosophical conversation about whether the concept of nature applies more widely, so that its extension includes some ethically non-neutral things. Within philosophy today there are well known debates about whether we ought thus to broaden our construal of the concept of nature. A handful of moral philosophers who write about the relationship between humans and animals—most prominently Cora Diamond and Raimond Gaita—effectively lay claim to this broad understanding of nature, representing humans and animals as natural, worldly beings that we require moral imagination to understand. And these moral philosophers are in the company of a wide range of artists—think, for example, of literary authors such as J.M. Coetzee, Marilynne Robinson and W.G. Sebald, filmmakers such as Werner Herzog and Marsh, and painters such as Sue Coe—whose work demonstrates the cognitive power of moral imagination, its necessary relationship to ethical understanding of humans and animals. The work of these moral philosophers and artists represents a direct challenge to the work of animal advocates who restrict themselves to hard concepts of human beings and animals. Yet these animal advocates rarely discuss or even acknowledge the challenge.

•

To see the point, consider a further example: Jonathan Safran Foer's 2009 book *Eating Animals*. Safran Foer's book has a clear political agenda. He undertakes to expose the brutality of the industrial farming of land and sea animals and to convince readers that support for such farming is unacceptable. But he also praises a number of farmers who attempt to preserve traditional methods of animal husbandry. Although he doesn't endorse any particular methods of raising and killing animals for food, he also doesn't exclude the possibility of finding methods he can wholeheartedly sanction. This openness makes his position insupportable to those activists who advocate the complete abolition of relationships in which animals are treated as things that can, for instance, be eaten. But what matters for my purposes is not whether his political agenda is radical enough but the range of methods he uses to open our eyes to features of animal life to which many of us are blind. Along with statistics and other information, *Eating Animals* also contains many literary devices designed to engage readers' moral imaginations. At one point Safran Foer tells us that while the details about the contemporary meat and seafood industries "are important ... they won't, on their own, persuade most people." Referring to the sorts of literary gesture characteristic of his own writing, he then adds, "something else is needed."

In one passage, Safran Foer presents a traditional Filipino recipe for stewed dog. Just before this passage, Safran Foer has been describing scenes from his life with his own pet dog George. He acknowledges that different cultures form tight bonds with different animals, and hence that he is taking for granted the perspectives of his own culture, in which dogs are looked upon as having a kind of precious vitality.

The recipe for stewed dog starts like this. "First kill a medium-sized dog, then burn off the fur over a hot fire. Carefully remove the skin while still warm and set aside for later use." These lines depend for their power and interest on our already regarding dogs in the non-neutral manner just mentioned. They encourage us to think anew about familiar conventions for preparing meat by getting us to contemplate them in reference to what we already recognize as the precious lives of dogs. "Cut meat into 1 inch cubes," the recipe continues. "Marinate meat in mixture of vinegar, peppercorn, salt and garlic for 2 hours." This recital is supposed to get us to shudder at the thought of cubing and marinating the flesh of dogs. At the same time, it invites us to look upon other animals as we look upon dogs, so that we are struck by the idea that when we eat other meat we are doing something analogously shocking to what we would be doing if we cooked and ate dogs. Safran Foer's efforts here are directed toward imparting a certain cognitive content—namely, that what we are doing when we eat animals is *this* shocking thing—and his efforts depend for their success on eliciting a certain activity of moral imagination. Like Marsh, then, Safran Foer appeals to moral imagination as a way of helping us to understand aspects of the lives of animals.

Not *every* appeal to moral imagination succeeds, of course. There are plenty of stupid, manipulative and even corrupt works about animals. On the other hand, even animal advocates who remain committed to viewing the world as "hard" can admire the output of a Marsh or a Safran Foer. What they cannot do, though, is conceive of imaginative artistry as anything more than a flourish that, however provocative, is in principle separable from a work's underlying content. And that is what I am urging. We should break from these thinkers in allowing that works like *Project Nim* and *Eating Animals*—works that call for the exercise of moral imagination in reflection—may directly contribute to our understanding of animals' lives, thereby laying the groundwork for more effective and clear-sighted animal advocacy.

CHILDREN AND ANIMALS

by David Egan

I didn't know it at the time, of course, but the older sister who directed most of my childhood games was a future novelist. A special incantation transported us to Fairyland, where the rooms of our house became the chambers of a mighty castle, the backyard bristled with the whispers of elves and fairies, and a walk in the woods offered half-glimpsed insights into the deepest mysteries. Fairyland was a world of make-believe: I *made* myself believe that all these things were real. My five senses told me I was still in the same old house and that all the characters in Fairyland bore a striking resemblance to my sister. But my sister helped me along: borrowing the rhetoric she'd picked up in church, she informed me that if I couldn't see these worlds—if the elven forest looked like my backyard—that was the fault of my own lack of faith. My feelings of guilt were excruciating. I still remember the day that my sister—grown a bit older and less patient with these childish games—informed me that Fairyland didn't really exist. I might be projecting a little, but I think that was the day I stopped believing in God.

But maybe belief doesn't enter into it at all: I was *playing* at Fairyland, not investigating its veracity. Belief fits into a world where some things are true and others are false, and where the aim is to buy into all of the true ones and none of the false ones, while complying dutifully with the laws of logic. Disregarding these laws, I ran around in both my backyard and the courtyard of a fairy castle at the same time. For play demands acceptance, not belief: I didn't have to suspend my disbelief to accept the truth of Fairyland any more than athletes have to suspend their disbelief when they accept that a bunch of chalk lines drawn on the ground place certain restrictions on their movements. Children accept that Santa Claus delivers gifts on Christmas Eve and the Easter Bunny deposits chocolate eggs in the garden because that's part of the game. Only later does it occur to them to ask whether Santa Claus or the Easter Bunny is "real."

•

Most stories written for children between the age of learning to speak and the age of doubting Santa Claus—it varies from child to child, but roughly between the ages of two and eight—seem to feature animals that talk, wear clothes, and inhabit human-like family and social structures. Why?

One answer would be that children are passive consumers of whatever stories adults shovel their way, and that adults impose zoo-centrism on children. But children are hardly passive recipients: they beg to be told favorite stories again and again, and refuse to sit through stories that bore them. If you're the kind of person who won't believe anything social-scientific studies don't tell you, trust me, the studies have been done and kids show a strong preference for stories with talking animals. Parents who tell their children only realistic stories won't condition their children to respond positively to realism. They'll just bore their children.

Anyway, children's stories aren't the only tales that swarm with talking animals. We find a similar anthropomorphic menagerie in myths. In fact, myths and children's stories share a lot more than just talking animals. The central conflicts lean heavily on binary oppositions like good/evil, security/fear, life/death and so on. The storytelling has a strong rhythmic component, employs vivid imagery and delights in the fantastic. Ancient myths also evince what we find in oral cultures today: nonliterate people, like children, outstrip literate adults in their fluency with metaphor. Studies show that three- and four-year-olds can generate a wider range of appropriate metaphors than college students can.

As far as we can tell, myths also elicit the same spirit of make-believe as children's fantasies. The Haida tell the story of Raven releasing the first people from a clamshell on Rose Spit beach on the northeastern tip of Graham Island, but in telling this story they're neither reporting a supposedly factual occurrence nor weaving fiction. Their attitude toward their myths—or at least their attitude before contact with Europeans—was no more true-or-false than my childhood attitude toward Santa Claus.

A strict distinction between fiction and reality, where it makes sense to talk about belief as endorsing some things as true and rejecting other things as false, goes hand in hand with literacy. The mid-century classicist Eric A. Havelock describes the massive cognitive shifts that take place when we start to relate to language as something written and not just spoken. For nonliterate people, speaking is a kind of acting that takes its place alongside other kinds of action. Literacy sets the reader apart from the world of action, says Havelock, and that distance makes more room for relating to the world in terms of knowledge and belief rather than action alone. In a world where stories are heard and not read, they become a part of that world. When we encounter them in books, stories have a separate existence, which makes it more natural to compare them with the world and sort them into fact and fiction.

Where acting in the world means being a part of it, contemplating the world means being apart from it. At least it does for us: nonliterate societies and preliterate children do their contemplating in the middle of things, as one part of a living, breathing world. Making sense of things involves embodying them, feeling what it would feel like to be a tree, a bird or a rock. (Bear in mind that it isn't just animals that myths and children's stories anthropomorphize: Thomas the Tank Engine is as much a person as Winnie the Pooh.) Everything in the world is given the benefit of the doubt: it's as much like us as our imagination can allow.

Literacy permits a degree of detachment from the world, and that also means a degree of distance from other animals. Like us, dogs breathe, move, make noises, have desires and lusts and emotions, and they even think; but dogs aren't particularly prone to detached contemplation. If you aren't either, you have less reason to think of yourself as essentially different from a dog. From totem to Tigger, the oral imagination seems a lot more inclined to identify powerfully with animals. Before we can think of ourselves as having dominion over the beasts, we live among them.

It might sound like I'm recapitulating all those awful colonial stereotypes of the savages as children who need to be civilized by the benevolent adult hand of European reason. Is this comparison between mythic cultures and preliterate children horribly condescending? They say all stereotypes have at least a grain of truth to them, and the truth here is that non-literate adults and preliterate children do share some things that literate adults lack (there are also—obviously—many, many differences). If this sounds condescending, to my mind that reflects a condescension toward children that's far more pervasive and taken for granted than any condescension toward nonliterate societies. Children aren't incomplete, unformed adults: they're complete, fully formed children, and the transition from childhood to adulthood isn't simply one of progressive improvement any more than the transition from oral society to post-industrial civilization is. Both involve trade-offs and compromises—and imagination is one of the main casualties.

•

If we drop the assumption that childhood is simply an imperfect version of our literate, rational adulthood, we start to see children as distinctive and peculiar creatures in their own right, creatures whose powerful identification with talking animals should come as no surprise. One talking animal from adult literature—the ape Red Peter in Kafka's "Report to an Academy"—gives some hints as to why. Kafka has Red Peter address a learned society, recounting the story of his astonishing journey from an African jungle to "the average education of a European man." Peter takes his name from a red scar on his cheek, left by the first of two shots that incapacitated him and landed him in a cage on a steamship bound for Europe. Peter quickly recognized that the only way out of his awful confinement was to learn to imitate his human captors and win their acceptance. So begins the arduous, painful task of suppressing his animal impulses and learning human language and manners, which culminates in his finding "a special way out for me, the way of humanity."

In *The Lives of Animals,** J. M. Coetzee's protagonist Elizabeth Costello tells her audience that she feels like Red Peter, and she says she doesn't mean this ironically. Costello sees Red Peter not as a scholar addressing his peers, but as "a branded, marked, wounded animal presenting himself as speaking testimony to a gathering of scholars." Red Peter's wound is that first shot by which his animal self was confined and which forced him to seek a "way out" by becoming human. He exhibits this wound not just in the literal sense that he bears it on his face, but also because his ability to address the Academy in the first place is a consequence of that wound: learning to speak like an educated European was the only alternative to confinement and abuse. A novelist uncomfortable in an academic setting, Costello feels herself similarly wounded in the forced acquisition of scholarly decorum. She contrasts the rigorous cogitation of the Academy with "fullness, embodiedness, the sensation of being," and suggests that, in suppressing this fullness, we also suppress our feeling of kinship with other animals. Costello sees Kafka and Red Peter, and, by extension, herself, as "monstrous thinking devices mounted inexplicably on suffering animal bodies."

She never says as much herself, but Costello's characterization applies, I think, to all of us, or at least to all of us some of the time and some of us all of the time. Red Peter tells his

---

* Also published as Lessons Three and Four in *Elizabeth Costello.*

audience that he has only the dimmest recollection of his life before he awoke in a cage on the steamship, and similarly my own memories vanish into a haze as I reach back deeper into the training that, among other things, taught me to string written words together like this. Writing about my life as a child is curiously different from writing about my life as a college student: it's not just that it's farther in the past, it's also that, in a very real sense, I was *someone else* back then. We are born hairless apes with certain aptitudes for imitation, language acquisition, play and so on, and our elders gradually train us into humanity. This process of domestication is inevitably violent, even if this violence isn't necessarily wrong: acculturation requires rigorous discipline, and as many sticks as carrots.

But it's at least as true to say that we play our way into adulthood as to say that we're trained into it (and both of these ways of putting it, I think, carry a lot more truth than saying we're *reasoned* into adulthood). Childhood is a period of intense and incessant play. We fiddle with toys and exposed electrical sockets, we imitate every animate being in our environment—as well as those in the richer menagerie of our imagination—and even practical activities only make sense to us as games. A spoonful of food is more likely to land in a child's mouth if it imitates an airplane on the journey over.

And adulthood begins as a game. The characters my sister and I played in Fairyland were usually teenagers and adults (even if sometimes elven teenagers and fairy adults) because we were drawn to these older role models in their authority, self-possession and freedom. What child hasn't played some version of House, where the roles of father and mother, professional and wage earner, find enthusiastically inept imitation? Children play out the roles they imagine themselves one day

assuming. Because my sister built many of our games around the heroes she most admired in stories, princesses were often the most dynamic protagonists. I think my parents took it pretty well when I said that when I grew up I wanted to be a princess.

In playing our way into adulthood, we play our way from nature to culture. The opposition between nature and culture is one of the commonest binary pairings that structure children's stories. Max is banished from the culture of the dinner table and travels to the land where the Wild Things are; a wardrobe in an English country house leads Peter, Susan, Edmund and Lucy into the alfresco world of Narnia; Babar moves between the cultured world of the city and his original home in the jungle. The nature/culture contrast is particularly potent for children who are born as little apes and play their way into cultured humanity. As children, we know we aren't just animals, but we also know that we don't fully belong to the perplexing, ordered world of grown-ups. We're a lot like clothed, talking animals, somewhere betwixt and between. No wonder Peter Rabbit made a lot of sense to me as a child.

Adults aren't the only ones who feel nostalgia for childhood: a seven-year-old boy is more keenly aware than a grown-up of the childish things he's left behind with his five-year-old self. Children look up to the adults they're learning to be, but they aren't blind to the irony that, in playing House, they're playing at being people who play far less than they do, and have far more responsibilities. We only dimly grasp these responsibilities as children, and look upon them with understandable anxiety.

The semi-cultured animals of children's stories often face challenges that speak to the anxieties of growing up. These animals are almost always prey, and where they aren't, they certainly aren't predators: bears often feature as protagonists in children's stories, but they never eat anything more human-like than a fish. (Alex the lion in the animated film *Madagascar*, who struggles with his carnivorous instincts when he finds himself in the wilds of Madagascar with his herbivorous friends, is the exception that proves the rule). Consider the Three Little Pigs, pursued by the Big Bad Wolf who wants to eat them. When you reflect on the animal most known to eat pigs—at a rate of some one hundred million metric tons per year—it isn't hard to see who the Big Bad Wolf stands in for. The house-building pigs are slowly finding their way into the world of adult humans, but this world also threatens to gobble them up.

•

As a child, I rooted for the Three Little Pigs as well as for Wilbur in *Charlotte's Web*, and I delighted in the company of Piglet. I also ate ham sandwiches for lunch. I never really thought twice about this odd tension. And not because I was unaware: there was never a moment of shock when I discovered that ham (or pork chops or bacon) was *pigs*. Beatrix Potter understood that children could

see pigs as both people and food at the same time: in *The Tale of Little Pig Robinson*, she summarizes and dismisses the eponymous hero's aunts as follows: "Aunt Dorcas was a stout speckled pig who kept hens. Aunt Porcas was a large smiling black pig who took in washing. We shall not hear very much about them in this story. They led prosperous uneventful lives, and their end was bacon." Much as I neither really believed nor disbelieved that Fairyland or Santa Claus were real, I neither really believed nor disbelieved that the delightful piggies I encountered in stories were the same animals that passed through my digestive tract.

Well into adulthood, I held on to the conflicting views that animals were my fellow creatures and that animals were my food. The delight I feel on encountering real-life pigs isn't just a holdover of fond feelings toward the storybook pigs from my childhood. Those fond feelings themselves arose from a sense that's dimmed as I've grown older: that I, too, am an animal, and that the similarities between pigs and me are more important than the differences. That grown-ups can see animals both as fellow creatures and as food reveals that we don't entirely leave behind the childhood ability to accept incompatible beliefs. But the imaginative contradictions of childhood play are also gentler: there were no slaughterhouses in Fairyland.

reviews

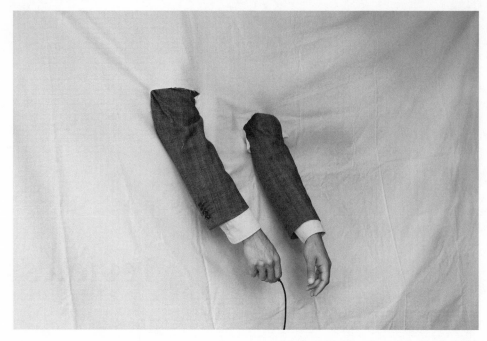

Herbert Weber, *Formal Approach*, 2007

MAD MEN

by Jacob Mikanowski

D ON DRAPER IS watching his wife Megan get ready to film an ad for Baxter shoes. She's dressed in a mock-European folk costume consisting of a canary blouse, scarlet dirndl and floral headdress. It's ludicrous, like a parody of Snow White (the ad's motif is Beauty and the Beast), but she looks great in it. And while she's filming, Don watches her with a look of, well, what exactly?—is it amusement, pride, satisfaction, contempt? As usual with Don it's hard to tell. Except for rare moments of intense emotion, Jon Hamm's face is a mask. The camera follows him as he walks out into the empty soundstage surrounding the set in a beautiful slow tracking shot out of *Sunset Boulevard* until the set shrinks into a point of light. The camera pivots and then catches Don again as he's walking into a vaguely Oriental-themed bar while the theme to *You Only Live Twice* plays in the background. Don orders an Old Fashioned. A beautiful woman approaches him, asks for a light. Then she points to a friend at the other end of the bar who wants to know, is he alone?

After five years we should be used to this, but still: what a tease. TV is generally a fairly transparent medium—conflicts get stated up front, characters announce why they're doing what they're doing, something moderately exciting happens before every ad break. But at its best, *Mad Men* remains admirably opaque. Characters' motivations remain unstated and unexplained, their emotional reactions uncertain and subject to endless interpretation. Does that final question mean that Don is really alone, and that by giving in to Megan's ambitions he has severed his connection to her? Or had he already lost her before, when he played a reel of her screen test for himself in a replay of the famous Carousel scene from Season One, and saw the flicker of an emotion that already existed only in memory, and on film? Did he give Megan the audition to spite her mother, or because he felt sorry for her? What does it all mean for the future? Is Don about to go back to his tomcatting ways, and be with Megan like he was with Betty? Is he alone and desperate, or fulfilled and free? And what is the rest of the gang going to be doing in 1968?

One of the great things about *Mad Men* is that the end of each season holds the seeds of the show's future. This year featured Timothy Leary, the Chicago Nurse murders, the Texas Sniper, George Romney, the Rolling Stones. Next year I see Megan in Paris, appearing as an extra in Jean-Luc Godard's *Weekend* or on the barricades during the May events. Roger will be in India, up in Rishikesh with the Maharishi Mahesh Yogi and the Beatles, or in Marrakech with a bag of bad hashish. Joan will have left it all for the West Coast, hiding a gun in her purse for her Black Panther friends and scoring a bit part (quotes, unattributed) in one of Joan Didion's high-class hippie-kickings. Don will be selling the two great American incendiary devices—napalm and Richard Nixon. Or maybe he'll take a job with the Democrats and be the third person on the left when Sirhan Sirhan shoots Bobby Kennedy in the Ambassador Hotel. Shaken, he'll hole up in a Topanga Canyon bungalow with a starlet and a stack of Pocket Poets paperbacks until her new friend Charlie knocks on the door...

It's all possible, but in all likelihood the next season is going to start the same way as every other season, inside the Sterling Draper Cooper Pryce offices, centered on the lower-case drama of chasing accounts and hiring staff. *Mad Men* belongs to the new generation of long-form programs characterized by big plots, complex character arcs, and patterns of foreshadowing and symmetry spanning years. But among the shows of the so-called TV revolution—*The Sopranos, Deadwood, Breaking Bad, The Wire*—*Mad Men* is an outlier. For one thing, it's the only one of these shows that isn't principally about organized crime. As a result it's much less violent, and often much slower, in terms of plot, than its peers. Compared to the spectacular, bloody confrontations on those programs, the world of *Mad Men* tends to be pretty mundane. Events on the show center on office relationships, romantic entanglements, and the season-to-season business of the advertising agency. An entire episode can be devoted to Don having a cold or taking a trip to a Howard Johnson with his wife, and a whole season can hinge on getting the account for Heinz baked beans. In fact, it's remarkable just how compelling the show makes the actual business of making and selling ads. Where the high points of the other programs involve fratricidal murders or assassinations, many of *Mad Men*'s strongest scenes revolve around pitch meetings—the Lucky Strike "It's Toasted" campaign, Belle Jolie lipstick, Jaguar, and most indelibly, the Kodak slide projector or Carousel.

That pitch, which takes the form of an unexpectedly moving monologue about the etymology of nostalgia, ends with Don comparing the slide projector to a time machine: "This device isn't a spaceship. It's a time machine. It goes backwards, forwards. It takes us to a place where we ache to go again." *Mad Men* works in a similar way, taking viewers back to a nostalgic, beautiful past, fulfilling a yearning we didn't know we had. Through its immaculate art direction, the show presents an incredibly desirable world, a self-contained bubble of late-Fifties fashion and retro vice made out of, in no particular order, Brooks Brothers suits, glass partitions, whiskey tumblers, vintage Cadillacs, narrow ties, pomaded hair, elevated busts and sherbet-colored dresses.

The outward beauty of *Mad Men* can suggest a certain moral glibness. For several critics, this surface is the source of the show's appeal and the root of its failings. It's a costume drama, or a soap opera in period clothes. For Jenny Diski, the historical recreation itself is too perfect to be convincing: "The style of the Sixties in *Mad Men* is so relentless and polished in every detail that it actually deals a death blow to authenticity." Other critics fault the show for what they take to be an ironic distance between the politics of the past and those of the present. In this view, *Mad Men* works by satisfying the self-regard of its viewers, inviting them to gawk at the repellent norms of a vanished world. Daniel Mendelsohn, writing in the *New York Review of Books*, finds its attitude towards the past "simultaneously contemptuous and pandering." It's an exercise in hypocrisy, "a kind of dramatic having your cake and eating it, too," while for Mark Greif the whole show is merely "an unpleasant little entry in the genre of Now We Know Better."

But if *Mad Men* does do a better job than actual advertising at making alcohol look refreshing, cigarettes pleasurable and sex enticing, it's because its characters recognize that those things are beautiful, and make life worth living. And although it's true that the characters on *Mad Men* move through a glamorous haze of cigarette smoke, brown liquor, and sex which makes their frequent moral lapses—apt in any given episode to include racism, treachery, callousness, indifference, smugness and lechery—seem not only forgivable, but attractive, that's only because of the depth of our identification with them. Devoted watchers of the show forgive them their faults, and condemn them for their cruelties. Why would we expect them to act better than we act now, or to lack prejudices that still exist? Who are we to take credit for the fact that we know now not to smoke when we're pregnant? I've never felt superior to any of the characters; I just want to spend time with them, and dream alongside them. Who doesn't want to be Don, or Roger, or Joan? Or Peggy. Especially Peggy.

Mad Men invites sympathy in complex and often contradictory ways. Like many people, I waver between Don and Peggy, but the show keeps the door open for a host of others (who could have guessed that of all the characters Daniel Mendelsohn would find Glenn, the sweaty neighborhood Holden Caulfield, to be the most compelling?). This play of identifications is something novels do. And because of it, like a novel (and unlike a tragedy) *Mad Men* is able to tell a complex story about the past, in which every step forward involves a series of tradeoffs, unforeseen consequences and painful sacrifices. Beneath its layers of vintage décor and television cliché, *Mad Men* is a story about history, and possibly the closest thing we have in the culture to a historical epic.

G EORG LUKÀCS SAID that the historical novel, in its classic nineteenth-century form, was "an epic depicting a transformation of popular
life through a set of representative human types whose lives are reshaped by
sweeping social forces." The great transformation of popular life tracked over
the course of Mad Men is the entrance of women into the workforce. Slowly, and
with a gradualness that only novels and long-form television can afford, Mad Men
is taking us through this revolution in American social life. It wasn't something
that happened all at once; the percentage of women employed doubled between
1940 and 1980, and only rose by some fifteen percent over the course of the
1960s. Nor was this process synonymous with the emergence of feminism as a
philosophy or a political movement. Instead, it was a phase in a tectonic shift
in the structure of American society. It's the kind of movement that changes
everything it touches but only registers retroactively in its full dimension. Mad
Men treats this shift with an impressive deal of nuance. It shows the changing
terrain; as the field expands, different strategies open up. Each of the women on
the show—Peggy, Joan, Megan, Betty—belongs to a slightly different generation
and each navigates the field of opportunity in a different way. Watch the men
with one eye, and the show is a boozy boardroom version of Glengarry Glen Ross,
all competition and banter with a mild twist of male melancholy. Watch it with
the other eye, as a show entirely about women, and it's Hedda fucking Gabler.

It takes a while for this to become apparent. Notwithstanding occasional
excursions, the characters on Mad Men live in a closed world. History, as we generally define it, in terms of political events and social transformations, only occasionally intrudes. The Sterling Cooper partners briefly work on the 1960 Nixon
campaign. Kennedy's assassination disrupts the wedding of Roger's daughter.
The Ali-Foreman fight becomes the inspiration for an ad for Samsonite luggage.
The Vietnam War shows up mostly on television. Before Season Five, the Civil
Rights Movement barely featured; then it was addressed through an episode of
race baiting at a rival agency and the hiring of a black secretary named Dawn.
For most of the show, though, life at the offices of the Sterling Cooper agency
is a sort of ancient regime before the fall. The offices are a stage for mid-Fifties
kabuki, a bubble erected to allow Roger Sterling to relax in a perpetual martini
swoon, Bert Cooper to pad around in his socks and examine his antique Japa-
nese erotica, while Joan manages the secretary pool like a busty prison guard
from Women in Cages.

Of course, not all characters are created equal. Many of the players are
made to fit a type. Lane Pryce, the English accountant who helped save the firm
from the clutches of British shareholders (played by the superb Jared Harris), is
the schoolboy out of water. Pete Campbell, junior account executive, is a greasy,
entitled striver with a Napoleon complex; a casual rapist, office pimp, and an

uptight prig, he skulks around the office like a WASP Iago. (A pure villain, there to hate—and yet, his reading *The Crying of Lot 49* on the train to work made me want to like him. Speaking of which, Don reading Frank O'Hara made me love him—who cares if he's really more of a William Carlos Williams kind of a guy.) Ken Cosgrove, his less interesting rival, is a cheery but flint-hearted man of many talents, who spends his nights writing short stories about maple trees and existentially depressed robots. Paul Kinsey, the most notable of the copywriters besides Peggy, was a pipe-smoking fop and would-be White Negro who sounds like he crawled out of the faculty lounge of a Kingsley Amis novel. Long my favorite, he was banished for two years before coming back this season and trying to hustle spec scripts for *Star Trek* while in the clutches of the Hare Krishnas.

Then there's Don Draper, the creative director of SDCP and the center of the show. In the first episode Don comes across as a weirdly handsome blank. Born Dick Whitman, the son of a small-town prostitute, he was brought up by a stepmother who despised him and watched his father die in front of his eyes after being kicked by a horse. In Korea, he stole the identity of his commanding officer after a freak battlefield accident, later hustling his way into a job at Sterling Cooper by tricking Roger while he was drunk. By the time we meet Don in Season One, he's the agency's leading asset and rainmaker. He's like Cary Grant, without the self-deprecation or inner distance, or Clark Kent if he were trapped in a Richard Yates novel. He's a suburban husband and compulsive philanderer, a man in a gray flannel suit with a taste for foreign film matinees. If Don were to narrate his own life, it'd be full of hard bitten self-pity. He sympathizes with Nixon, "Abe Lincoln from California," and Sonny Liston over Muhammad Ali. At the same time, he's capable of moments of deep empathy (or is it pragmatic understanding?) with people from different backgrounds. He's the self-made man who is also a cipher, a hustler, a man from nowhere, a self-invention and a mask, the rebel conformist. He's a figure from American literature, and American myth—at different moments Melville's confidence man, Cheever's swimmer, Dick Diver, Coleman Silk from *The Human Stain*, Rock Hudson as Ron Kirby in *All That Heaven Allows* and his double life outside of it.

But if Don is a myth, and the other male characters on the show are brilliantly executed types, Peggy belongs to history. It is Peggy who absolutely refuses to accommodate herself to what's expected of her—doesn't acknowledge her child; won't be pressured into anything by her boyfriends; would rather work all night with Don. Joan Harris, the voluptuous office manager, marries a handsome idiot who rapes her before leaving for Vietnam. In the past season opportunities have been dangled before her—she briefly reads scripts for the television department and becomes indispensible to the financial operations of SDCP. But ultimately she only acquires power by trading sex for it. At the end of

Season Five the partners (except for Don) persuade her to sleep with an oleaginous car sheikh in exchange for five percent of the company as part of a bid to win their first car account. Meanwhile Megan Calvet, Don's new wife, succeeds effortlessly at advertising, winning the Heinz bean account with a bravura pitch over dinner. But when she quits the agency to try her hand at acting, she finds herself stymied without her former connections. Towards the end of Season Five she's increasingly adrift and lost, on the edge of artistic failure and feeling herself increasingly to be little more than an object for Don's sexual attention.

Betty, Don's first wife, is more of a challenge. She starts the series battling depression and the ennui of the left behind. Over time, she's treated as a neurotic, demeaned for her childishness, made to seem cruel and infantile. Unable to see past a horizon of men in her life, she uses her children for validation and spite. This season she barely figured at all, except for a brief cancer scare brought on as a result of some rapid weight gain. As she's given a moment of tragic awareness, Betty becomes briefly sympathetic, but before the episode is over the danger passes and she is revealed again in all her childishness.

The relationship between Don and Peggy is at the heart of the show. It is less the story of a suppressed romance than of a quest for mutual acknowledgment. The ties that hold them together—mentorship, money, emotional dependence, creative collaboration—are all tacit, and involve libido only indirectly. In the economy of the show, Peggy is Sister Carrie to Don's Jim Gatz, until she turns into Girl Friday. Over five seasons she rises from an abject, exploited secretary, expected to take care of the sexual needs of her bosses to a copywriter and now the creative director at another agency. In the beginning, she's repeatedly humiliated in the office, subject to frank sexual appraisal by the men and catty one-upmanship by the women. Seduced by Pete, she gets pregnant without realizing it; after the baby is born she refuses to acknowledge it. Don visits her in the drab municipal hospital were she's interred (did she have a breakdown?) and tells her that this never happened, offering her a way forward—after all, he knows about reinvention.

Over time, Peggy goes from being Don's charity case to being his protégé and, finally, his secret sharer. The shift in power between them culminates at the end of Season Five. Belittled by Don and frustrated by her diminished role in the agency, Peggy decides to quit SCDP to become the creative director at a rival agency. The scene in which she announces her decision to Don is one of the most powerful in the whole run of the show. In a few instants, Don shifts from bravado to pleading to acceptance to grief. After he kisses Peggy on the hand, we realize that it has been a kind of love affair after all.

S O WHERE DO they go from here? We don't know what's going to happen with most of the characters, but Matt Weiner has tipped his hand pretty heavily about what Peggy will be doing next year. When she runs into Don in a movie theater, she tells him that she's been asked to come up with a name for a new women's cigarette (the same cigarette was already in development at the end of Season Four, when a consultant promised to get a meeting for SDCP with Reynolds after they lost Lucky Strike). Presumably this is going to become the famous Virginia Slims "You've Come a Long Way Baby" campaign. These ads featured short vignettes set in the early part of the twentieth century in which harried housewives grind meat and chop wood for their mustachioed husbands, occasionally sneaking away for an illicit cigarette while a voiceover explains how different things were back then: "It used to be lady, you had no rights. No right to vote, no right to property, no right to the wage you earned." "Civil Rights were for men only. Such as, drinking. Such as, smoking." The scene then switches to the Sixties present. As the theme jingle plays, modern, liberated, smoking women stride confidently toward the camera in modern dress, which c. 1968 involved astounding combinations of candy-striped leggings, diaphanous pastel robes and pentagonal capes. (It may seem oddly regressive for a series of advertisements celebrating women's liberation to feature models who look like escapees from a futuristic harem, but then again, no one sings about the nineteenth amendment anymore either).

Peggy's involvement in the Virginia Slims campaign will bring at least one motif of *Mad Men* full circle. The first episode of the show begins with Don dreaming on his couch, searching for the inspiration that will turn into the "It's Toasted" slogan for Lucky Strike, long the agency's biggest and most important client. Don's original insight was to realize that it didn't matter *what* quality was used to this end—all cigarette tobacco is toasted, but once that trait was claimed for Luckys, it becomes distinctive and useful. Peggy's realization promises to be larger: you can sell cigarettes by selling America. Smoking and drinking can be civil rights, just as much as voting. Any movement that starts as a drive for liberation or equality will eventually end up as a way to sell soda.

In the fourth episode of the second season, Don says something strange. After a plane crash in New York (which kills Pete's indolent father), American Airlines comes to SDCP to try and save their image. Don says to forget about the past: "American Airlines is not about the past any more than America is ... throw everything out ... There is no such thing as American history, only a frontier." Peggy's answer seems to be that history is America's advertisement for itself. It's the story we tell ourselves to sell the world on America, and to sell ourselves on

Virgina Slims "You've Come a Long Way Baby" campaign

a promise. So in a sense, the Virginia Slims campaign is *Mad Men* in miniature, and in reverse.

Mad Men may look like an ad—and it even does an ad's "job" of arousing and inflaming desire in its viewers (as anyone throwing a *Mad Men* party or contemplating Christina Hendricks or Jon Hamm knows), but it is, at heart, a sly sort of historical chronicle. The show's ability to incite passion indiscriminately may be part of what makes critics so nervous about *Mad Men*—after years spent reading pop culture like Roman augurs, studying the entrails of defeated shows for a path into the zeitgeist or a sign of the demise of capitalism, its blatant seduction must seem either dangerous or put-on. But even as *Mad Men* sells us on a shimmering vision of mid-century vice, it's also telling us a story about our past, and our present. And it will be especially fitting if Matt Weiner lets Peggy have the big self-reflexive epiphany about the show. She's always been more than a wounded, moral, ambitious foil for Don. She's our everyman, the little Balzacian figure leading us through the labyrinth of the past. She understands Don's point about American history being a frontier better than he does. There's no history; only marketing. It isn't a time machine; it's an ad.

FURTHER EVIDENCE

by Luc Sante

1. There is something uncannily familiar about this view. It's as if you've been here before.

2. But probably the familiarity is generic. You've experienced a scene resembling this one. In photographs, necessarily.

3. The immediate details are not in question, although you know all these items intimately. Here you know the setting from life and the cars from the movies, as if the memory of your actual youth was beginning to drift backwards into history.

4. It's a landscape that makes sense to you, a place you could just enter and inhabit. You know that sort of garage, even that kind of tenement, although nowadays they are probably hidden under asphalt or vinyl siding.

5. Or here, you take in a scene that is clearly outside your experience. This is what trash looked like before plastic, wood, metal, brick, maybe rubber tubing. Even so, you are familiar with the trash-strewn backyard; the details dissolve in the overall effect.

6. You imagine, rightly or wrongly, that the pictures were taken in New York City. Something about proportions, primarily. Architecture, too, but architecture that is to a greater or lesser degree dictated by scale, New York City being more constricted than other cities.

7. But there is something else going on here. Look at the scale of these pictures, their depth, their focus on an unoccupied middle distance. It is as if each of them is a stage set for a play that has been and gone or maybe has not yet occurred. In each of these pictures what is most notable is a central lack, an absence, a void.

8. In other words, these are scenes of crimes. As a photographic subject, the scene of a crime is unusual in that its presence can be embodied in its absence. To hijack Randall Jarrell's definition of the novel, a crime scene photograph is an unremarkable depiction of an unremarkable view that has something wrong with it.

9. Very often the only hint we have that a photograph depicts a crime scene is that the subject is of such a staggering banality that it would be difficult to think of any other reason for its photographic depiction.

10. Sometimes the image teases the eye, suggesting clues that may well dissolve upon closer examination. Sometimes the focus is deliberate and concentrated, but it is not always clear when it is simply the result of ineptitude.

11. Sometimes crime scene pictures can resemble nature photography, but without the presence of nature. Very often the scene is as near to a blank canvas as is possible without fading entirely into nothingness.

12. When Walter Benjamin compared Atget's photographs of city streets at dawn to crime scenes, he was primarily referring to the similar quality of absence. But there is a difference. Atget's subjects are of interest in themselves; his pictures are unpopulated so that the viewer will not be distracted from the aspect to which he wants to draw the viewer's attention.

13. In these pictures, on the other hand, there is no such inherent interest. The point of focus can only be on what is missing. It is a bit like Sherlock Holmes's dog who failed to bark.

14. Each of these photographs is a signpost, featuring a giant illuminated arrow pointing to an empty field. If you come upon such a picture, bereft of any context, you will find yourself helplessly looking for a clue, a hidden statement, a punchline.

15. You will ransack your mental image bank looking for precedents. You will pick up and discard snapshots and film stills that perhaps connect on matters of randomness and architecture but to very different effect.

16. You will consider social documents, such as the chronicles of tenement life made at the beginning of the twentieth century by such photographers as Jacob Riis, Lewis Hine and Jessie Tarbox Beals, but human beings were never absent from those pictures.

17. You will think of the sort of pictures made to advertise or document real estate, but, like any advertising use of the medium, those are pictures meant to flatter, a task at which these photographs utterly fail.

18. You may remember seeing pictures taken for tax surveys, although those tend to home in on some specific sorts of information and favor a broad scale over a narrow focus.

19. Even assuming that the inhabitants of these spaces owned cameras, it seems unlikely that they would have taken this sort of picture for their own amusement or nostalgic contemplation.

20. And although it is not utterly out of the question that the press might have taken an interest in some of these scenes, the pictures are simply not of the professional quality of press photographs.

21. They appear to be amateur photographs, taken with professional equipment, of scenes that are too neutral to be private and yet somehow too loaded to be public. It is clear that, whoever they were meant for, they were not intended for us.

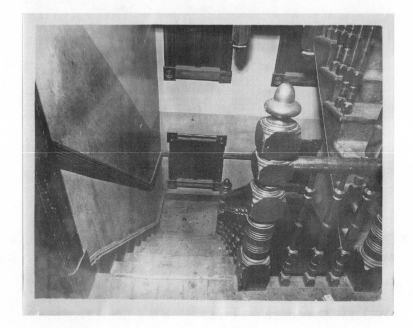

22. By process of elimination, then, you are left with only one conclusion: that they are photographs of crime scenes, and that they were taken by members or employees of the police whose interest in the photographs cannot have been more than narrowly professional, if not altogether expedient.

23. In 1992 I published a book called *Evidence*, occasioned by my coming upon, in the New York Municipal Archives, a collection of evidence photographs taken mostly by members of the NYPD's Fingerprint and Identification division between 1914 and 1918.

24. I had been looking for historical photographs of slum life in New York City, not an easy task beyond the well-known pictures by Riis, Hine and Beals. I certainly hadn't expected to find those pictures, which shocked me, haunted me, showed up in my dreams, and would not leave me alone for months after I initially stumbled upon them.

25. They imposed a hundred questions. The appended information in the archives was fragmentary at best. Who had taken them, and why? How had they managed to achieve that style? And wasn't it frivolous to even consider such a thing as style when looking at photographs of victims of violent crimes?

26. I had to know everything about the pictures, about what they showed and who took them and under what circumstances, and while I was often frustrated in my investigations, I found enough hints to be able to piece together some of the stories, at least.

27. The pictures certainly changed my relationship with photography. I had long been interested in the medium, but I had never written about it and hadn't thought very hard about its meaning and significance and relation to truth.

28. The pictures made me look harder, first of all, and imposed the task of trying to look with a historian's eye and a detective's eye and an eye for certain off-register kinds of beauty, all at once. The contradictions coiled up in those photographs effectively presented me with a syllabus which I would have to take on if I wanted to be able to untangle them.

29. Take the matter of style, for example. Those pictures from the teens had a certain very specific look to them, even though I eventually discovered that they were made by at least four, and as many as seven, different people.

30. It was a question of equipment, lens and lighting above all, in combination with the random and sometimes apparently whimsical application of a deliberate method for documenting crime scenes, established in the late nineteenth century by Alphonse Bertillon.

31. What I had taken for a style proved to be the result of an array of circumstantial factors, involving happenstance, laziness, hierarchy, bureaucracy, inconsistency and spatial and technical limitations.

32. In any case that look was indelible. I saw evidence photographs from Paris taken right around the same time, and while the generic similarities were obvious, the look was not the same. And neither were evidence pictures taken a few years later in other cities. Every city—New York, Paris, Los Angeles, Mexico City, Sydney—seemed to have its own distinct... what?

33. "Style" was not the word. For one thing, even beyond the apparent moral hazard implied by such a term, it was unconscious. Could we call it a "fingerprint," a "profile," an "m. o."?

34. The available language appears loaded, but for good reason. The connection is not idle. Detectives are in the business of detecting patterns of display or behavior that the parties themselves are oblivious to.

35. Criminal investigation is in effect an intense critique of style, which subjects people, places and things to a relentless examination,

36. every homicide detective as rigorous as the most exacting scholar or curator or impresario or fashion buyer or grant-panel judge,

37. lavishing such attention most often upon people, places and things that would not otherwise be the object of such scrutiny.

38. As a consequence, criminal investigation is uniquely suited to supply a broad range of answers when we want to know how people lived,

39. since most crime scenes are rigorously ordinary, since crime can occur anywhere, all the way from the front parlor to the crawl space under the stairs,

40. since people do not have the opportunity to clean up for company, since crime and economic standing are so effectively intertwined, since until recently most crime victims were not of a class able to afford to record their lives photographically.

41. So it is that the archived remnants of criminal investigations of the past are superior if usually neglected anthropological documents, containing incidental information that often cannot be found anywhere else.

42. But because these are also photographs, members of a category of object that also includes confections and fashion statements and works of art, we can confer aesthetic values upon them that were never intended by anyone connected with their making, but which are no less real for all of that.

43. Style is not an end point but a process, one that the photographer sets in motion but that is provisionally completed by whoever looks at the work, so that the meaning of style in a photograph remains in flux.

44. It is changed by us, and it will be further changed by our successors. Like homicide detectives, we learn to recognize patterns, often by intuition and without necessarily even being able to name the connecting thread of a given pattern.

45. The more pictures we see, the more patterns we store in our back brains, and today a child has seen many more photographs than even an alert and curious adult would have a century ago. Thus we are able to recognize the beauty and meaning in pictures from the past that would have been obscured to their contemporaries by sociological circumstances.

46. That is why our photographic pantheon can now include such disparate figures as Anna Atkins, Solomon Butcher, E. J. Bellocq, Eugene de Salignac, Frederick Glasier and Mike Disfarmer—photographers who in their day remained unknown or unrespected, considered at best as competent artisans, at worst as dog-and-pony exhibitors. We do know better than our predecessors.

47. In the course of preparing my earlier book, I happened upon a manual of criminal investigation written for detective buffs, which included a couple of tiny reproductions of photographs that, despite their size, I knew at once had been made by the NYPD in the earlier half of the twentieth century.

48. A couple of years ago I was on eBay, scrolling through the Photographic Images, pre-1950, as I do from time to time, when I had a very similar experience. There on the left-hand margin was a thumbnail of a picture that I was immediately certain had been taken by policemen in New York City.

49. It was one of a lot of seven assorted photos, some interesting and some not, some competent and some not, that had been taken some time after the subjects of my book but earlier than 1950, apparently in New York City but not in Manhattan, to judge by the building stock.

50. The information given by the seller was scant to nonexistent. They were identified as crime scenes, it is true, but I hardly needed to be told. They were original prints, which was interesting since the pictures in my book had been preserved only as glass-plate negatives. The wide range in print quality indicated a variety of hands had been involved.

51. Eventually I bought about a hundred pictures from the same source, an old woman whose father had been a police detective in Brooklyn. I didn't succeed in getting much information from her. She was alternately vague, kittenish and obdurate. She didn't know, and she didn't want to know.

52. I nevertheless pestered her with questions for months. I wanted to know, for one thing, why there were no bodies in the pictures. It turned out she did possess a number of photographs of murder victims, but she was holding out for more money, and implied she had a line on some well-heeled collectors, perhaps hoping to spark my competitive zeal.

53. Eventually I got her to send me some scans. The results came as a relief, in a way, since I was not tempted to spend beyond my very limited means, but overall they came as a disappointment. The pictures were brutal without mystery. They simply looked like illustrations from the detective magazines of the period.

54. Whatever circumstances of equipment and procedure connected these pictures to the ones in my book did not hold for the photographs involving corpses. The ones pictured in 1914 had often appeared to be in a state of grace. These did not. They were simply dead. The difference may have simply been a matter of lighting, of the burst and decay of the magnesium powder as opposed to the sustained and pitiless interrogation of the flash bulb.

55. In the meantime I still had many questions. The backs of the photographs told me a few things. There were exactly two dates in the entire lot: 1931 and 1937. In addition, a legible license plate was a World's Fair special, 1940.

56. There was one noted address, on Bond Street in the Gowanus district, and four specified precincts: the 68th, which still covers Bay Ridge, Dyker Heights, and Fort Hamilton; the now-defunct 82nd, which included Gowanus and parts of South Brooklyn and Brooklyn Heights; the 83rd, in Bushwick; and the 92nd, also decommissioned, which straddled Bushwick and Williamsburg.

57. There are a handful of case numbers indicated, but the likelihood of my finding records of them is exceedingly slim since the New York Police Department has not preserved those records. The stories are gone.

58. But then the debris is also gone, and the furniture is gone, and the buildings may be gone and maybe even some of the addresses. The people are long gone. What's left are shards of unknowable stories. Here and there we can imagine arson or burglary, perhaps assault. There are no bloodstains or weapons.

59. There aren't even a lot of personal effects visible in these pictures. The people of the 1930s were far less likely to decorate their walls than their predecessors of two decades earlier, while at the same time they owned more furniture and stowed away more of their belongings, so that the pictures are less valuable as historical records.

60. And you couldn't call the photos cinematic, a popular adjective for crime scene photos. They might as well be going out of their way to be anti-cinematic, showing you the backsides and armpits of everything, and tilting up to the ceiling and down to the floor like drunks or people with stiff necks.

61. The pictures are sordid. They are intensely private. They respond to questions with blank stares if not outright hostility.

62. They do not draw interesting anecdotes in their wake, do not reward the questing eye with unexpected rich details in their backgrounds and margins, do not offer even a whiff of period color.

63. These are photographs of agitation. They are about all the places you look when you're desperate. You're looking for where to climb into the house, where to hide the evidence,

64. where to start the accelerant, where to find the party you want to shake down, where to look for the money, rumor has it, hidden somewhere on the premises.

65. They are ugly, uncooperative pictures, as if they themselves were suspects being given the third degree at the station house. They are pictures of beatings and bruises applied to objects and structures.

66. They do not permit even a whiff of the romanticization that documents of crime are often accused of perpetrating. They were not meant for you or me, and they maintain their omertà.

67. But that is not where their interest ends. It is where it begins.

68. They are objects of mystery, enigmas sealed by their very banality. They are so obdurate they might as well be sculptures. They will never crack.

ROOTABAGA COUNTRY

by Megan Pugh

For a few decades, Lyndon Johnson's proclamation that "Carl Sandburg was more than the voice of America ... He was America" seemed almost believable. The young Socialist newspaperman from Illinois had grown up to be a comforting, white-haired bard who assured the nation of its greatness. He won three Pulitzer Prizes: one for the fourth of his five-volume biography of Abraham Lincoln, and two for his poetry. He visited both John F. Kennedy and Johnson in the White House. He received honorary degrees from at least 28 universities, and over two thousand people attended his 75th birthday party. His celebrity reached such heights that in 1966 his publishers released a glossy coffee table book of photographs: Sandburg gazing across the family farm, Sandburg meeting foreign ambassadors, Sandburg playing guitar, Sandburg dancing with Marilyn Monroe, Sandburg posing with a bust of Abraham Lincoln.

Carl Sandburg was once an icon on the order of Mark Twain, but these days he can seem like a mere footnote in American literary history. To critics committed to the heroics of modernist experimentation, Sandburg's poetry is embarrassingly sentimental, a relic of overwrought populism that reads like a bad imitation of Whitman. It is rarely taught in the academic circles where tastes are made and canons are formed.

Even further off the critical radar are Sandburg's American fairy tales. In 1922, Sandburg published *Rootabaga Stories*, and soon followed it up with *Rootabaga Pigeons*. It's *Rootabaga Stories'* ninetieth anniversary, a milestone that—though the books remain in print—has gone unnoticed, probably because the stories are marketed to children. But these stories aren't really just for children. They target the entire nation, reimagine it, and give it back to us in startling forms. Rootabaga Country is a shadow-world of America, where characters we've never encountered—Dippy the Wisp, Lizzie Lazarus, Blixie Blimber—seem as mythic and familiar as Paul Bunyan, Pecos Bill, and Johny Henry.

Paul Bunyan and Pecos Bill are, of course, American folk heroes—men whose strength and vigor supposedly helped build the country. But if the *Rootabaga Stories* are exercises in nation-building, they also tear the nation apart. Rootabaga Country is governed by absurdity as well as by justice, by tragedy as well as by whimsy. Sandburg may have looked like a comforting old bard in that coffee table book, but here his work is brazen and strange, as tense and fresh as it must have felt to readers ninety years ago.

I N THE TEENS and Twenties, Sandburg steeped himself in national legend, and when he wrote *Rootabaga Stories* he'd already begun collecting the folksongs that would make up his 1927 collection *American Songbag*. He tended to end his poetry readings with songs, bringing out his guitar to perform old standards like "Frankie and Albert," "Jesse James" and "Boll Weevil." There are no boll weevils in Rootabaga Country, but there is agricultural disaster: a heat wave makes the all the corn on the Huckabuck Family's farm pop, and they must flee through deepening white drifts. There are cultural disasters, too. In the city, a man convicted of sneezing "in the wrong place before the wrong people" is sentenced to hang. (Sandburg doesn't use the word "lynching;" he doesn't have to.)

Indeed, in Rootabaga Country, hardship is never far away. As one character says, after hearing about a woman so confused about whether to take a clock or a looking glass on her trip to find true love that she never leaves home: "It is a strange story. It has a stab in it. It would hurt me if I couldn't look up at the big white clouds shouldering their shoulders, rolling on the rollers of the big blue sky." The speaker claims to have escaped the stab, but we don't believe her. The clouds, like nonsense words, point only at themselves, distracting us from hurt without undoing it.

The spinner of most of the tales in Rootabaga Country is the Potato Face Blind Man, an old-fashioned music physicianer who sits in front of the post office with a beat-up accordion, healing the world with his stories and his songs. He warns against backsliding, as when he tells Blixie Blimber about a man who won't fix his "slipfoot" and keeps losing what he's going after—a cautionary tale that prompts Blixie to go home and do her chores—but Potato Face also relishes the more basic pleasures of sound, sharing "the song the mama flummywisters sing when they button loose the winter underwear of the baby flummywisters." When Potato Face gets lonely, he plays the blues, "the sleepy song of the long wind going up the sleepy valleys," inventing an existence where he has "time and money to dream about the new wonderful accordions and post offices where everybody that gets a letter and everybody that don't get a letter stops and remembers the Potato Face Blind Man."

Potato Face wants a world that doesn't neglect him and he wears a sign, "I Am Blind *Too*," to remind the public of its shortcomings. But he is a generous beggar, accepting charity in receptacles designed for the needs of almsgivers. He has a thimble for tiny dimes, a larger cup for people who enjoy throwing coins at a distance, and a mug with a hole in it, "for the very poor people who wish to give me a nickel and yet get the nickel back."

Figures like Potato Face reveal Sandburg's lasting concern for those on the margins of American society. When they show up in his poetry, they sometimes become tokens, actors in a grand historical pageant. But in Rootabaga Country, Sandburg's vision of populist acceptance is bound up with verbal and imaginative play that saves it from didacticism. The citizens of Rootabaga Country are too restless and complex to reduce to type.

In "The Wooden Indian and the Shaghorn Buffalo," for example, statues in front of a tobacco store and a haberdashery come alive in the moonlight and ride together to the wilderness. An Irish cop who witnesses the metamorphosis describes it later: "I was sitting on the steps of the cigar store last night watching for burglars. And when I saw the Wooden Indian step down and the Shaghorn Buffalo step out, and the two of them go down Main Street like the wind, I says to myself, marvelish, 'tis marvelish, 'tis marvelish." The policeman's accent comes out at the moment he expresses his awe, as if to underscore the idea that being an immigrant helps him understand the desire to escape to a freer land.

That restless yearning also drives "The Two Skyscrapers Who Decided to Have a Child." The buildings want a "free child" who can—in words that echo "America the Beautiful"—"run across the prairie, to the mountains, to the sea." But their son, a high-speed train, dies in a crash that also kills his passengers. In desperation, the ornamental sculptures on top of the skyscrapers leap to their death on the street below. The story closes: "One was a tin brass goat. The other was a tin brass goose. And they lay next to each other." Industrial progress may be designed for a free and expansive nation, but here it falls short. And so, in an odd way, does metaphor: man may have designed those tin brass animals to embellish the tops of his towering buildings, as symbols of power, whimsy or both. But in Rootabaga Country, symbols have wills of their own. They suicide as they break free.

All manner of objects change forms in Rootabaga Country, as in "How Pink Peony Sent Spuds the Ballplayer Up to Pick Four Moons," where the sportsman climbs trees to bring the woman he loves moons that are caught in the branches. On the ground, each moon takes on a new, ornate identity, becoming "the silver hat full of peach-color pearls, the circle of gold with a blood-color autumn leaf, the brass pansy sprinkled with two rainbows, the Egyptian collar frozen in diamond cobwebs." At dawn, they shrink into less glamorous adornments: four oranges holding four yellow silk handkerchiefs that, years later, will warm the necks of Spud's and Peony's four children. The story is a commentary on the artistic process: you try to capture beauty, but it keeps escaping your grasp. When you finally get a hold of it and try to share it with other people, what started as communication ends up as accessory, providing ornament and comfort without the assurance of permanence.

The citizens of Rootabaga Country are desperate; they long to break out of the confines of their own lives. Rats guide a group of travelers through a snowstorm to found the Village of Liver and Onions. Broken jugs of molasses transport three boys with secret ambitions to a miniature world. Gimme the Ax and his children, tired of a life where "everything is the same as it has always been," sell all they own, tie their spot cash into a rag bag, and march to the train station to buy a ticket "as far as the railroad rails go and then forty ways farther yet." Their journey opens the first collection of stories as it opens new lands; after traveling through nations of balloon pickers and pigs with bibs, they reach Rootabaga Country.

If all this sounds like the American frontier, it should. Gimme the Ax is part hobo, part pioneer and part pilgrim—an American hero meant to displace the kings and queens of European fairy tales. In *Rootabaga Stories*, Sandburg creates a fictional folklore that's at once surprising and iconic, without lapsing into utopian wish-fulfillment. Instead of a perfect nation, we get a disarming picture of people on the move. Transformation can be scary.

Sandburg's images are so striking, his cadences so hypnotic, that you can't help but remember the stories quickly, and soon you feel you must have known them all along. The titles are a joy to read aloud: "How Six Pigeons Came Back to Hatrack the Horse After Many Accidents and Six Telegrams"; "How Henry Hagglyhoagly Played Guitar With His Mittens On"; "Shush Shush, the Big Buff Banty Hen Who Laid an Egg in the Postmaster's Hat." When these jangly, nursery rhyme rhythms give way to a more hushed tone, you feel like you've been let in on a beautiful secret: "Maybe you will hear the corn fairies going pla-sizzy pla-sizzy-sizzy, softer than an eye wink, softer than a Nebraska baby's thumb."

But the secrets aren't always gentle—as in the best folksongs and tales, darkness lurks close behind the rhythms: Frankie may go to the electric chair for shooting her lover; John Henry will die with a hammer in his hand; Potato Face may stay hungry; Rags Habakuk may sell his lucky blue rats and plunge his family into poverty; your neighbors may disappear; your home may not be your home. These possibilities are what make Rootabaga Country into such a remarkable reflection of America. The stories echo, but they won't let you settle down.

Kate Shay, *Untitled*, 2012
Instagram (@justthegritty)

BURNING MAN

by Clarisse Thorn

WHEN I WAKE up at the hotel in Reno, my memories are a messy pastiche. I reach for an image to encapsulate my experience of Burning Man, but everything I grasp feels like a cliché. Dancing beside a fluorescent art deco bus and a fire-belching metal octopus. Bonding with a new friend by solving a maze's secret doors. Randomly encountering a fake film crew composed entirely of trenchcoated noir buffs, who welcome me into their game. Accepting, with gratitude, the recitation of a poem about self-awareness and another about kissing. Walking to the edge of a desert dance floor to stretch and greet the dawn with an exhausted grin.

Each of these is all of it, and yet the smallest piece. So I'll start at the beginning.

I AM IN A garage with a neuroscientist, a sales executive, a teacher, a bike co-op manager, and some dude whose deal I don't know. Me? I'm a feminist sex writer specializing in S&M and moonlighting as a new media consultant. We're loading a truck with toolboxes, barrels, bicycles and more. This camp's theme is watermelons; the garage is strewn with watermelon umbrellas, and we pack in a bike rack painted to look like a giant watermelon slice. Unknown Deal Dude doesn't recognize it for a full minute. "Ohhh! It's supposed to look like a watermelon!"

"Maybe that's a sign that the theme has become too abstract," I say to Bike Co-op Manager.

"Maybe it's a sign that it's become abstract *enough*," he says serenely.

I wander into the back and pick up a plastic bag full of sequined watermelon pins. "Where did these come from?" I ask the teacher. She shrugs. In the corner, someone is wrapping a cooler packed with dry ice in a Mylar space blanket. The plan, apparently, is to transport an ice cream cake to the desert. There will also be many watermelons.

The executive is "working from home" during the 40-hour drive, using a batch of car chargers and a cellular uplink. As he clicks away on his laptop, we discuss the philosophy of social networking sites; the neuroscientist's latest research on rat brains, and her anxieties about handling her undergraduate mentees; the people in our lives who we wish we hadn't lost touch with; the ethics of eating human meat; plus the spiritual usage of psychedelic drugs. I learn a new phrase: "thinky thoughts." The Co-op Manager tells me it describes "thoughts one has on acid that *seem* really deep, and *are*."

A few hours in, we pull up at the "World's Biggest Truck Stop." I wander through the place with Unknown Deal Dude. We are floored and astonished by this culture clash. I am so floored that I text my best girlfriend.

> **Me:** Sold here: wolf and horse t-shirts; confederate flags, "don't tread on me" snake flags, "mess with the best die like the rest" US marine flags; John Wayne DVDs; auto tags for "redneck girl"; infinite self-help books.
>
> **Her:** I've been there OMG.
>
> **Me:** Is there any vegan food?
>
> **Her:** Haha.
>
> **Me:** Fritos it is!
>
> **Me:** Dude, on the way out I noticed the door says "support independent truckstops."

I emerge, slightly shell-shocked. "That place is confusing," I say to Bike Co-op Manager.

He grins. "Confusion is an important state of mind."

B URNING MAN BEGAN in 1986 when the founder Larry Harvey decided, on a whim, to burn a wooden man on a San Francisco beach. Five years later, Harvey had acquired some dedicated co-conspirators and the event had morphed into a bigger, artier free-for-all in Nevada's Black Rock Desert. Twenty years after that, it's a world famous camping-out festival that drew over 50,000 attendees in 2012.

I first heard about it as an internet junkie in the Nineties; one of my online friends enthused about the explosions and gun usage, another about the drugs. Apparently, when the Burner population got too large and a basic "no gun" rule was instituted, some folks felt this was an unacceptable infringement of their freedoms that made it not worth going anymore. But plenty continued to attend, and the sheer size of the crowd led to further regulations and infrastructure. This included the development of a circular layout with street signs, a medical station, a Department of Mutant Vehicles, a post office, radio stations, an airport, etc. The year 2000 marked the creation of the Temple, which became one of the most important structures: a space to meditate, reflect and mourn. The temporary city of Burning Man—which is only fully-realized for a single week per year—is called Black Rock City.

In 2004, Larry Harvey tried to pin down Burner culture by laying out "ten principles." These are:

> **Radical Inclusion:** Anyone is invited and welcome.
>
> **Gifting** and **Decommodification:** The event is devoted to "unconditional gift-giving." Thou shalt not engage in commercial transactions, sponsorships, advertising or barter.
>
> **Radical Self-Reliance:** "Burning Man encourages the individual to discover, exercise and rely on his or her inner resources."
>
> **Radical Self-Expression:** Do as thou wilt, but don't hurt anyone.
>
> **Communal Effort** and **Civic Responsibility:** Collaborate, cooperate and take care of each other. Oh, and don't break the law.
>
> **Leave No Trace:** Don't hurt the earth, and especially not the federally-protected environment of the Black Rock Desert.
>
> **Participation:** "We make the world real through actions that open the heart."
>
> **Immediacy:** "No idea can substitute for this experience."

There are critiques to be launched. So many critiques. Perhaps those of you who share my Advanced Degree in Social Justice Snippiness, claws honed by hundreds of internet catfights, spotted critiques in my first few paragraphs. For example, while Burners may Leave No Trace upon the surface of the desert, an awful lot of fossil fuels are burned to get there. Scarce resources are used when, say, transporting an ice cream cake in a dry ice freezer. And my Spidey sense for "Third World exploitation" was tweaked by those cheap, beautiful, mass-produced sequined watermelon pins.

Plus, the Burning Man organization charges for tickets, which arguably puts a cramp in Radical Inclusion. To be fair, the event has enormous costs to cover, like a $750,000 land usage permit. There are also "low-income" tickets available for a mere $160 apiece (most 2012 tickets ranged from $240-$420), but the bigger individual costs are equipping oneself and getting there. You can already see certain demographics represented in the crew I drove out with—and in our reaction to the World's Biggest Truck Stop. All my campmates had degrees from prestigious universities, including a doctor and a Google engineer. I can count on one hand the number of people of color I met at the event.

According to statistics from the 2010 Burning Man census, 20 percent of Black Rock City makes over $100,000 per year (compared to 6 percent of the U.S.A.'s general population). A bit over 30 percent of the city makes under $30,000 (compared to a bit over 50 percent of the general population). As a writer, I myself wouldn't have gone if my journey weren't heavily subsidized and I hadn't been given a free ticket by generous, well-heeled friends. And let's face it: I may not be at my friends' earning level, but I'm still in their social class. Offering me that access isn't nearly as Radically Inclusive as offering it to Joe the Plumber would be. But here we have the perennial problem of class segregation: none of us know Joe the Plumber.

Burning Man came from San Francisco, and to San Francisco doth most attendees return. The period between 1986-2012 has seen San Francisco shift from hippie beach town to the mecca of Silicon Valley. If a bomb hit Black Rock City, then the Valley would need a new crop of CEOs. My understanding is that even the art of Burning Man reflects this evolution. The hippie and radical sex elements remain, but attendees who have watched for ten years say it's shinier now, costlier, with an "engineered" feel to it.

A worthy comparison might be the super-hippie Rainbow Gathering, which began as a late-Sixties San Francisco group but first came together in 1972. The Gathering moves from forest to forest each year, is free to attend, does not have a single leader at the helm, and is considerably more working-class than Burning Man. There are fewer artworks at the Gathering, and more environmental problems; the Burning Man organization purchases a permit that helps the government deal with its impact on federal land, something the Rainbow Gathering has apparently resisted. On the other hand, the Gathering seems to help genuinely down-and-out folks, like marginalized homeless kids.

With all that said: our Advanced Degrees in Social Justice Snippiness are important, but if I lay mine aside for a moment, I can't help liking Burning Man. A lot of things are just plain cool, like the art. I love the whimsy of bringing an ice cream cake, even though it uses lots of resources. But most importantly, despite my considerable grumpy skepticism, the festival keeps surprising me.

O UR DRIVING CREW pulls ridiculous shifts and we nap in the back of the van when we're tired, refusing to stop, like teenagers. I've got the last shift driving, but everyone's awake as we pass into cloud-grey desert with steel-blue mountains behind it. I've only attended once before—2010—so I keep quiet as veteran Burners note landmarks, like the guy selling "Indian tacos" with a handwritten sign by the side of the road. Last stop before Black Rock City is Gerlach, which Wikipedia describes as a "hamlet." Population: less than 200.

The main watermelon camp organizer applied for Early Access passes so our crew could enter the gates of Black Rock City and build some stuff before the event officially begins. We turn off the road soon after Gerlach, and our tires instantly kick up dust on the playa—the ancient dried-out lakebed that forms the Black Rock Desert. Playa dust is a phenomenon unto itself, permeating every aspect of life in Black Rock City. Absent unusually wet conditions, the dust swirls and eddies at every turn. It whitens dark garments, chokes bike chains, corrodes electronics and occasionally slams the city in blinding storms that can last for hours.

Burners carry goggles and masks and scarves, but the dust still clots eyes and throats. Playa dust is dry, weirdly sticky and highly alkaline; overexposed skin can crack unless it gets moisturizer and lemon baths. Despite my best efforts to filter my air, I contracted pleurisy (a lung ailment) this year. Two years ago, I got a sinus infection. As for hair, unless it's braided, the wind and dust can convert it to dreadlocks in days. The term of art is "playafied."

Obviously there's no water in the desert. There's also no food—and none is available for sale, because the Center Camp of Black Rock City sells only café drinks and ice. (Most proceeds are donated to charity.) It's barely possible to find internet or cell phone network access, so I put up an "out of town" email response before I left. My campmates and I have brought everything we need to survive—and will dispose of it, cleanly, afterwards. (The one exception is that the Burning Man organization provides ranks of Port-A-Potties.) Sunblock is crucial in the day but the night is very cold. The elevation is 4,000 feet, and it's normal to spend the first 24 hours queasy as the body adjusts. The common cold gets passed around like candy.

Building the city is a not a minor task. Teams of volunteers start big projects like the Temple several weeks in advance. This year, the Temple was designed by David Best, who also designed the first Temple in 2000. The 2012 version is an awe-inspiring, multi-tiered, Asian-looking structure in a courtyard 150 feet by 150 feet. Each piece is machine-cut, gorgeously intricate, like wooden filigree. Some production costs are defrayed by the Burning Man organization; Burners have also donated tens of thousands of dollars. Like the Man and much of the other art, the Temple will ultimately burn.

After we arrive, I help my friends at the watermelon camp set up for a while. Through a haze of dust and exhaustion, we hammer down stakes and page through the Black Rock City guide, where different camps have listed themselves and their offerings. The sales executive says, "Hey guys, here's a challenge: find the weirdest type of yoga class." We settle on Emotional Freedom Yoga.

Ian MacKenzie, *The Temple of Juno*, 2012

There are relatively tame events like tequila lounges or body painting or meditation or mask making, and more extreme ones like Double Penetration: Learn To Make Yourself Airtight. The musical emphasis is electronic, but events range from jazz to goth/industrial to a cappella dubstep. Oh, and karaoke, which I end up doing for five hours straight one day. (Don't judge.) There are thinky events: lectures on basic physics or international charity organizations, or Stand-Up Philosophy. Science-fictional ideas abound. I am transfixed by a lecture on cryonics, which is delivered by someone who seriously works in that field. Afterwards, I say to the speaker: "Do you think about Egyptian pharaohs a lot? You must think of them, like, constantly."

"Er... I *could*," he responds, and pointedly turns to another questioner.

Some camps are kind of like social services, such as the camp that does Coffee & Aspirin every morning. Or the Hiney Hygiene Station, where a polite and delicate gentleman will gladly don gloves and swab down your chafed nether regions. Not to mention the Human Carcass Wash, where people are trained to wash each other using a minimum of water and a maximum of respect: the event is not just a bath, it's a workshop on how to deal nicely with other people's personal boundaries. Some camps serve food or give other gifts, like Black Rock City postcards. And then there's Career Ending Footage: "Hate your crummy job but too pussy to quit? Get caught in compromising situations in our Career Ending Footage office."

There are also countless S&M classes, and several camps devoted to educating folks about polyamory (open relationships). I have friends and professional connections at some of them, and I keep meaning to stop by, but over the course of the week I never get around to it. I don't even make it to the class on jalapeño fisting, although I must admit I've never done that before. In fact, I end up attending exactly zero of the listed daytime events, except the one serving vegan coconut ice cream.

When sunset deepens the sky over the watermelon camp, I travel several blocks to find the friends I'll be camping with myself—some are old friends, and some are new. My camp is only fifteen people, and we're in such close proximity that we're bound to bond. My campmates have been on the playa for several days and have built shady hammock havens, a kitchen and a parlor. Just as importantly, they've done a lot of work on the camp art project. Pipe Dream is a twenty-foot-tall, two-ton, cube-shaped steel lattice of pipes; each is the width of an arm and capable of bearing many people's weight. It's basically a giant cubic jungle gym. I feel lucky that I know artistic, clever engineers as I climb to the center of Pipe Dream and help assemble a streamlined chandelier.

From the top of Pipe Dream, we gaze over the playa and the developing city. The streets are lined with teahouses and cinemas; everything lights up at night. There are lots of geodesic domes and, less romantically, RVs. The Man stands at the center atop a structure several stories tall. Most everything becomes more enormous and fantastical toward that looming figure.

We can't see it all from here, but I'll discover it throughout the week: a camp whose front is painted like a giant Tetris display; a roller derby with disco music; a life-sized ship, internal shelves stocked with books and bottles and lanterns, more intricate than a movie set, which appears to be "sinking" sideways into the playa; a full-size plywood maze with ladders, secret doors and misleading signs. This year's most political art project comprises several huge, satirical Wall Street buildings with logos like "Chaos Manhattan" and "Bank of UnAmerica." When they're burned, the project makes headlines from *The Huffington Post* to *Business Insider*.

There's a kind of stereotypical Burner fashion sense that meshes gender-bending, raver sparkles and playa practicality. I find myself thinking, *Oh, there's another man in a tutu with a many-pocketed belt and pink dreadlocks woven with LEDs.* There are plenty of exceptions, though, and in the streets and plazas and vast open space at the city's center, some Burners wear horse heads while others wear evening gowns. Or t-shirts. It's all good.

Those who feel tired of walking or biking can jump on a passing art car, which is usually easy because the speed limit is five miles per hour. In order to be allowed through Black Rock City, cars must be suitably whimsical and approved by the Department of Mutant Vehicles. Sometimes people just decorate existing cars or buses, but they are often far more ambitious. There's a car that looks just like a Western saloon, and several shaped like giant cupcakes. There's a magic carpet rippling a foot above the road, wheels hidden by tasseled fringe. My favorite art car is an enormous crouching dragon, each scale lined with red lights that occasionally shimmer blue. That one belches fire, of course, much like the tentacles of the rearing octopus-shaped car built from garbage cans. At night, when Black Rock City becomes dominated by techno clubs, many art cars boast DJs. (For my money—haha, see what I did there?—the best DJ set this year was a collaboration from Dr. Toast and DJ Ganucheau.)

T**HE RELIGIOUS RIGHT** is obviously displeased about Burning Man. One charming online rant calls the festival "Satan's Birthday" and blames it for the stock market crash plus various natural disasters. Lucifer is laughing at our self-immolation, apparently.

I was raised Unitarian, so this kind of imagery presumably doesn't resonate with me like it does for those with more traditional upbringings. But I discover it burrowing into my mind one night as I bike along the playa, weaving through hellish glowing clouds of dust, surrounded by topless revelers. LEDs flash, neon burns, everyone is wearing lights. Fire blooms everywhere I turn: fire dancers, fire sculptures. In 1996, the Burning Man theme was actually based on Dante's *Inferno*, and one of the founders played Satan. In 2007, Burner artists exploded 900 gallons of jet fuel and 2,000 gallons of liquid propane from an oil derrick, creating a mushroom cloud 300 feet high. (Perhaps ironically, the piece was intended to raise consciousness about environmental issues.)

Next to a huge geodesic-domed dance club, I run into a man I once met for a date in San Francisco. He has an elegant face, moves with perfect grace, and is so smoothly expressive that I can't bring myself to trust him. But I like him anyway—he's got a quick mind and does interesting technological charity work.

He's also got a way with his hands: he digs them into my back, and I breathe out slowly, my eyes closed against the pain. "The way you react when I play with you is interesting," he says. "Other women sigh with relief, or they ask me to go softer. But you hiss, like you've been dropped in hot water."

This particular dance-club dome has nets at the top: you can climb a tall ladder up the side, lie down and observe the dancers below, with nothing holding you but string. There's also a slide, and my graceful friend convinces me to try it. Naked terror freezes me in place when I reach the top. I wonder if I could survive an accidental fall. I'm shaking. I can't bring myself to slide down.

I take a deep breath, look out across the blazing dusty playa, at the brilliant art cars and installations lighting the horizon. The Man, outlined in neon, shines stark white against the night. I'm thrilled and extravagantly afraid. I think of Nero fiddling while Rome burned. I think, again, of damnation. I recently read about a study that found countries with a higher rate of belief in hell have lower crime rates; the same does not hold true for belief in heaven.

"No rush," says my partner below me, "it's not like there are lots of people coming up below us on the ladder." So I force myself onto the slide. At the bottom, I'm giddy with relief and throw myself into his arms. "It's extraordinary up there, isn't it?" he says. "Sitting on those nets is sitting on a thousand years of human history. Centuries of physics went into designing that dome."

"That's a nice way to imagine it," I say.

"How do you imagine it?"

I make a moue. "I don't want to think about it right now," I say. "But I find myself imagining the history in terms of war and suffering. The imperial global context allowing us to build a desert hallucination, while children starve in Africa." In another time and place, I'd feel self-conscious about my pretentious words. Right now I bury my face in his shoulder to banish my thoughts. Then I gaze at him, caught by the exquisitely balanced planes of his face. "Do you ever worry whether you're an angel or a demon?" I ask.

"I don't think about these questions the way you do," he says, putting his hands on me and clenching them. I arch into his grasp and whine a little. His eyelids go heavy, like a cat's.

"I'm going to call you Mephistopheles," I say.

He smiles. Lets go. My body feels abandoned; I wasn't ready for the pain to stop. "That's a long nickname," he says.

"Mephisto," I say. "For short."

"Maybe I'll get it tattooed on my knuckles," he says, and clenches his fists so he can playfully count off the fingers. "M-e-p-h-i-s-t-o."

A REVIEW OF BURNING Man would be incomplete without discussing drugs, especially hallucinogens. The event has ancestors in the San Francisco hippie scene, and is often compared to a giant rave; both subcultures are heavily associated with drugs. Most Burning Man art fits the genre of "visionary art," which Wikipedia describes as derived from "symbolism, surrealism and psychedelic art." Some of the more stereotypical examples I saw in 2012 were paintings by Android Jones and Alex Grey at the Fractal Nation camp, placed under a color-shifting light that dramatically changed their color balance, moment to moment. One piece showed an exploding head with fiery eyes. Another showed ornamented skeletal and muscular systems. When red-lit, they almost seemed to be different pictures from the blue-lit versions.

I should note that plenty of people come to Burning Man and don't do drugs. For one thing, it's against the law, as the Burning Man website and Survival Guide will remind you. There are police at the event and some are undercover. Some attendees allege that there are more police this year, in fact— perhaps because Burning Man is more popular than ever. Many Burners content themselves with alcohol, which is both plentiful and obviously legal. (And no, I don't understand why alcohol occupies this privileged cultural space, despite being described by *The Lancet* as eight times more dangerous than ecstasy.)

Speaking of drug studies, recent findings have documented the ways that carefully used hallucinogens can help with mind-body problems like addiction or Post-Traumatic Stress Disorder. It's not just researchers talking about them, either; when Apple founder Steve Jobs died, his *New York Times* obituary noted that he once described LSD as "one of the two or three most important things he had done in his life." Psychedelic drugs have never been mainstream, but we seem to have reached a pendulum-swing in the cycle where they're becoming less feared and reviled. Perhaps this is part of why Burning Man, too, has become a bigger deal in the mainstream. Of course it's probably more to do with its current connections to wealth and privilege and hyper-fashionable tech companies.

I don't personally believe hallucinogen use should be a free-for-all—any more than alcohol use should be. Or Ritalin for that matter. For every Steve Jobs or Hunter S. Thompson, there's a Charlie Sheen or a Cat Marnell. And even the "enlightenment" drugs—e.g. acid and mushrooms and ecstasy—are not *in themselves* a path to enlightenment. Yet when mixed with safe spaces and focused exploration and new ideas, they appear effective for some people. (Admittedly, the line between acid as a spiritual guide and acid as a party drug can be thin.)

I don't know how safe it is to request illegal drugs from random Burners; I've never tried. Conversation about drugs certainly is easy to come by, though. One event describes itself as: "Two nurses and a shrink share their knowledge about the true benefits and consequences of drug use. Come as you are and learn ways of ensuring that your drug experiences are fun and positive."

While watching a sunset from Pipe Dream, I talk to one guy who nonchalantly calls himself "very accustomed" to LSD. He tells me that, "There's Burner art you'll never understand if you don't take acid. Burning Man has refined the genre—art that causes aesthetic pleasure mingled with a 'What the fuck?' moment."

When I ask for an experiential description, he says, "Acid goes like this: first, my stomach rebels and food becomes puzzling. I know it's really kicking in when lights and fire become exceptionally interesting, and my skin gets happy and sensitive. Then my creativity leaps. I make connections faster than usual. I find many new metaphors. Hallucinogens never make me see things that aren't actually there; I merely put the world together differently."

A lot of people talk about Burning Man as being about togetherness, integrating with people. But it's also about integrating new experience: altered consciousness, altered states, altered perspectives. Many participants are intimately familiar with how hallucinogens can hurl them into explorations of personal and conceptual space, and accordingly the culture celebrates them. But they're not required. The sheer enormity of Black Rock City can swallow people in itself. While hiding in a shade structure during a dust storm, I meet a woman who says that when friends ask her about Burning Man, she tells them: "It's a lot like life."

MY FIRST YEAR at Burning Man, I was underwhelmed. I remember thinking: *Well, I can see how this festival would seem like a big deal to people who don't have access to alternative sexuality, or good dance music, or intentional communities, or hippies, or smart people, or fire art, or San Francisco.* Since I have semi-regular access to all those things, I was unconvinced that it was worth the considerable trouble and expense to see them in Black Rock City.

I also felt—and still feel, sometimes, despite my best efforts—some eye-rolling resentment at the "tourism" aspect. If this social experiment is so compelling, then why compartmentalize it? Why is it useful to question assumptions about cities, economies, social norms, if people leave those questions in the desert behind them? I once heard an aphorism that has always stuck with me: artists exist to take society's blame for the things we explore. Seeing things I love hemmed in so thoroughly makes me uneasy. Like we're being made into easier targets.

Yet I remind myself that people often need a safe and/or different space to try new things. Even I—now a pro S&M writer—had some of my seminal S&M experiences in distant cities. Something about drastic scene changes allows us to shake up our psyches. So although I'm uncomfortable with the idea that Burning Man is a utopia, there's something compelling about it as an inspirational pilgrimage.

In 2012, I deliberately avoid pre-scheduling; I also avoid things that I already know a lot about, and I find the city very different. The difference starts with a woman I dance with at one of the raver tents. She's a former dominatrix and teaches writing at a community college, so we bond right away. After an hour of conversation, she tells me and my companion that she has to run, but she wants to offer us a gift first: poetry recitation. She lets us choose from a list of five topics; my friend chooses "kissing" and I choose "self-awareness." The teacher throws back her shoulders and offers wide, dramatic gestures as she speaks. The poems make her eyes blaze.

On another late night, I'm walking back to camp when I come upon a group clad in khaki-colored trench coats and sunglasses. They've set up a small table with a rotary phone in the middle of an intersection. One is sitting in a folding chair with a megaphone; another holds a camcorder. As I watch, they flag down a passing couple. "You're late for your scene," exclaims the woman with the megaphone, who is wearing dark red lipstick. A dude with a huge pad of paper bounds forward and opens it in front of the bewildered couple; a classic film noir line is written on the first page, something about where the money's at. The group convinces the couple to play out a full scene, during which the rotary phone is a crucial prop. Then the couple departs, laughing.

Many onlookers have gathered. Two ask if they, too, can play a scene. The director becomes excited: "Wow, no one's ever *requested* to play a scene before!"

I watch the event over again with the new actors, and then ask the group if I can join. For a brief and glorious time I am their makeup artist, rushing up to recruits and brushing their faces with invisible cosmetics. (Some recruits decline to participate, but always politely.)

The next evening, I drop by the film crew's camp: a 1920s-style office with a picture-perfect iron lamppost, and Deus Ex Detective Agency stenciled on the door. They're hosting a speakeasy party in back, but I spend half the night being interrogated by a handsome detective in the office—until he turns the tables and puts me behind the desk to receive walk-in cases.

All this is undoubtedly awesome, and it's beginning to win me over, but I've seen it before. (I recommend the group Improv Everywhere for clever street-based pranks in major cities.) For me, the clincher pops up on my last day. The Burning Man organization sells ice at various locations across the playa, and every day someone in our camp volunteers to grab some for our coolers. I'm several blocks from Pipe Dream when I buy today's batch; I stagger outside with three full bags and look at my bike, realizing just how awkward and unpleasant this task will be.

Then an art car pulls up. It's decked with animal print couches, paisley hangings and Tibetan prayer flags. "Jump on," invites the driver, and climbs down to help with my bike. He also picks up two more ice-carrying dudes.

As I sink gratefully into one of the couches, a lady in a spangled white harem costume passes me a hookah full of grape-and-mint-flavored smoke. "We love doing ice runs," she explains. "It improves people's day so much when we offer them a ride, plus we get to explore the city."

I don't know if it was my own energy or the festival's in 2012—perhaps a combination of both—but it took a second visit to Burning Man for me to know the magic of it: *emergence*. Sure, there are brilliant artists, and some are world-class professionals. It's also true that this community is biased, that it is not perfectly inclusive or even-handed or open-minded. And plenty of people will experience Black Rock City as no more than an incredible rave, or meditational gathering, or place to find a hookup and experiment. Which is fine by me. The city is all those things, and those things are great (in moderation).

But what's better is that those things combine to create an inspiring stage for imaginative generosity, for cooperative art. It sounds so corny that I'm embarrassed to quote it, but as the Principle of Participation puts it: "We make the world real through actions that open the heart." Emergence is born from people choosing active engagement with a place that's designed to surprise. Black Rock City is the most total monument to creativity that I have ever seen.

O N MY LAST day I track down the poetry-reciting teacher at her camp so I can give her one of my books. (I bring six copies to the playa for gifts, and by the end I wish I'd brought more.) Her camp is called Love Potion; they distribute tiny two-dose glass bottles of herbal aphrodisiacs, to be shared with a lover. She ties a string around a bottle, then ties it around my neck. It's my only souvenir.

I arrived a little early and I'm leaving a little early, but right before I go, I watch the Man burn from Pipe Dream. The Black Rock City skyline is so vivid: most of the glowing art cars have gathered at the base of that familiar icon. Lasers spear across the sky. Fireworks spray. I'm not close enough to see them, but I know performers are twirling around the Man's base, many dancing with fiery hula hoops or fiery sticks or fiery fans. A few days after the festival ends, I will realize I'm not sure what the Man officially represents and call one of my campmates. "It's like an anti-establishment thing, right?" I'll ask. "As in: 'Damn the Man'?"

"Huh," she'll say, "you know, I've been going for years and I never thought about it. I guess I figured that the Man represents ego, and we're seeking ego-dissolution."

It will require fifteen full minutes of internet research to find an old, brief statement from Larry Harvey: "Representing nothing, the Man becomes tabula rasa: any meaning may be projected onto him."

Harvey, whose personality has been described as "messianic," recently announced his intention to oversee the spread of Burner culture throughout the world. Indeed, this is already happening: plenty of major cities, including Chicago, have Burner events year-round, up to and including camp-out "regional Burns." (This year, I heard about a South African regional Burn.) The Chicago community also awards a microgrant for community activism.

There's a funny phenomenon of wealthy people hiring experienced Burners to guide them around the playa, which one such guide defended by saying that "it makes rich, important people friendly towards Burning Man." Because so many technological innovators attend, some inevitably think up and field-test projects on the playa, like the inventor Vinay Gupta, whose cheap and durable temporary "hexayurt" shelters were first used in Black Rock City. Hexayurts are now standard in disaster relief. Burner art is increasingly placed in parks and museums.

I have reservations about Burning Man—more than most of my friends. I get impatient with people who can't see the class issues, and—call me a cynic—I suspect that this batch of activists and artists wouldn't have nearly the pull that they do if it weren't for the wealth of Black Rock City. If the difference between "high art" and "low art" is nothing but the difference in privilege between artists, then Burner art is turning into "high art" as we watch because its associated industry has gained so much status in our economy.

There's also the creepy cult comparison. One might wonder how long we have before we start seeing missionaries. (Please, somebody, write a post-apocalyptic science fiction novel in which Burning Man has become the state religion.)

Yet personally? I love the culture of Burning Man, and I love the creativity. And I look forward to seeing the culture spread, combine and recombine with new things.

On my way out of the city, I spot Bike Co-op Manager. "Did you have a good Burn?" he asks, and I nod. "It was better next year," he says; we grin at the standard Burner line, and give each other a hug.

THE POINT

COMING IN ISSUE SEVEN:

The Great American Think-Off

•

Socialism We Can Believe In (Part II)

•

On Christopher Lasch

•

Is Yoga Possible?

SUBSCRIBE AT

WWW.THEPOINTMAG.COM

$18 FOR ONE YEAR (2 ISSUES)
$32 FOR TWO YEARS (4 ISSUES)

BACK ISSUES AVAILABLE

LOVE IN THE AGE OF THE PICKUP ARTIST	THE CONSOLATIONS OF SELF-HELP	HARD FEELINGS	PREDATORY HABITS
"i first turned to the pickup artists after losing in love"	"it was my life coach who first introduced me to eckhart tolle"	"michel houellebecq has published four novels, all of them bitter and miserable"	"amidst nature's unreasonable scarcity, wall street often seems like a refuge of reason"

SOURCES

A PLEA FOR HUMAN FOOD

Michael Pollan, *The Omnivore's Dilemma*

Gary Taubes, *Good Calories, Bad Calories*

Henry David Thoreau, *Walden*

RETROMANIA

Jaron Lanier, *You Are Not a Gadget*

Simon Reynolds, *Retromania*

and *Rip It Up and Start Again*

and *Totally Wired*

SOCIALISM WE CAN BELIEVE IN

Janet Byrne, *The Occupy Handbook*

R. H. Tawney, *Equality*

and *The Acquisitive Society*

MY JOB SEARCH

Aristotle, *Politics*

Martin Yate, *Knock 'em Dead Cover Letters*

Girls (2012)

CAVE TROUT

Tom Regan, *The Case for Animal Rights*

Peter Singer, *Animal Liberation*

ON KILLING ANIMALS

Jeremy Bentham, *An Introduction to the Principles of Morals and Legislation*

Antonio R. Damasio, *The Feeling of What Happens*

James McWilliams, "PETA's Terrible, Horrible, No Good, Very Bad History of Killing Animals"

GETTING ANIMALS IN VIEW

J.M. Coetzee, *The Lives of Animals*

George Eliot, *Middlemarch*

Immanuel Kant, *Groundwork of the Metaphysics of Morals*

and "Conjectures on the Beginning of Human History"

Jeff McMahan, *The Ethics of Killing*

John Stuart Mill, *Utilitarianism*

USING ANIMALS

Gary L. Francione, *Animals as Persons*

John Locke, *Two Treatises of Government*

Mary Midgley, *Animals and Why They Matter*

Porphyry, *On Abstinence from Animal Food*

Henry Salt, *Animal Rights*

IMAGINATION AND ADVOCACY

Jonathan Safran Foer, *Eating Animals*

Project Nim (2012)

SEEING DOUBLE

J. M. Coetzee, *Elizabeth Costello*

Beatrix Potter, *The Tale of Little Pig Robinson*

CONTRIBUTORS

Charles Comey *is a Ph.D. student in the University of Chicago's Committee on Social Thought. His article, "The Passion of the Cow," appeared in issue 1 of* The Point.

Alice Crary *is a professor of Philosophy at the New School. She is the author of* Beyond Moral Judgment *(2009).*

David Egan *is a lecturer in Philosophy at Christ Church College, Oxford. He is also a playwright, and is currently working on a trio of short plays about the animals we eat, entitled* Three Little Pigs.

Justin Evans *is the Ennis Postdoctoral Fellow at Villanova University. His article on J.M. Coetzee ("Problems with Authority") appeared in issue 4 of* The Point.

Gary Francione *is a professor of Law and Philosophy at Rutgers and a co-founder of the Rutgers Animal Rights Law Project. His most recent book is* The Animal Rights Debate: Abolition or Regulation *(2010).*

Ben Jeffery *is a Ph.D. student in the University of Chicago's Committee on Social Thought. His essay for issue 2 of* The Point *("Hard Feelings") was later expanded into a book entitled* Anti-Matter: Michel Houellebecq and Depressive Realism *(2011).*

Heather Keenleyside *is a professor of English at the University of Chicago. She is working on a book entitled* Animals and Other People: Forms of Life in Eighteenth Century Literature.

Christine Korsgaard *is a professor of Philosophy at Harvard. She is the author of four books, the most recent of which is entitled* Self-Constitution: Agency, Identity, and Integrity *(2009).*

Jacob Mikanowski *is a writer living in Chicago. His art and literary criticism have appeared frequently on* The Millions *and the* LA Review of Books. *His review, "Cloud Gate, Tilted Arc," was featured in issue 5 of* The Point.

Megan Pugh *teaches American cultural and literary history at Berkeley. Her writing has recently appeared in the* Boston Review *and* The Believer.

Luc Sante *teaches writing and the history of photography at Bard College. He is a regular contributor to* The New York Review of Books. *His most recent book is* Folk Photography *(2009).*

Emilie Shumway *is a writer living in Chicago. She works at an arts-education nonprofit.*

Fabien Tepper *is a journalist with an M.S. in Animals and Public Policy. She is a resident writer at Mesa Refuge.*

Clarisse Thorn *is a feminist sex writer. She is the author of* Confessions of a Pickup Artist Chaser *(2012) and a collection of essays entitled* The S&M Feminist *(2012).*

WHAT IS *THE POINT* FOR?

- *The Point is for anybody who is frustrated with the intellectual poverty of the majority of today's journalism and public discourse.*

- *The Point is for serious, and seriously entertaining, essays on contemporary subjects like video games, steroids, self-help and Wall Street.*

- *The Point is for helping you think about your everyday life—how to parent, how to love, how to protest, how to read Marx.*

- *The Point is for reviews of new art, theater, literature and events— the kind you want to read long after you've seen or read the reviewed thing.*

We love publishing *The Point*, and we thank you for buying this issue and helping us keep going. However, we are a small print magazine operating in an environment that is not always hospitable to our brand of long-form writing. Our writers, our copy editors, our artists—we all work for free. With that in mind, please consider donating to *The Point*. We promise to use your money wisely to improve the quality of our magazine and to compensate our great writers.

If you have any questions, please don't hesitate to contact us by email at **admin@thepointmag.com**. Thanks again for buying *The Point*!

The Editors

Jon Baskin
Jonny Thakkar
Etay Zwick